Presbyterian Questions, Presbyterian Answers

Other Books by Donald K. McKim

Presbyterian Questions, Presbyterian Answers

Exploring Christian Faith

Donald K. McKim

Geneva Press
Louisville, Kentucky

Scripture quotations from the New Revised Standard Version of the Bible are copyright © 1989 by the Division of Christian Education of the National Council of the Churches of Christ in the U.S.A. and are used by permission.

Book design by Sharon Adams
Cover design by Night & Day Design

First edition
Published by Geneva Press
Louisville, Kentucky

This book is printed on acid-free paper that meets the American National Standards Institute Z39.48 standard. ♾

PRINTED IN THE UNITED STATES OF AMERICA

09 10 11 12 — 10 9 8 7 6

Library of Congress Cataloging-in-Publication Data

McKim, Donald K.
    Presbyterian questions, Presbyterian answers : exploring Christian faith / Donald K. McKim.— 1st ed.
        p. cm.
    Includes bibliographical references.
    ISBN-13: 978-0-664-50250-8 (alk. paper)
    ISBN-10: 0-664-50250-4 (alk. paper)
    1. Presbyterian Church—Doctrines—Miscellanea. I. Title.

BX9175.3.M37 2003
285—dc21

2003049191

With appreciation, love, and gratitude to
Rebecca and Ron Cole-Turner and Rachel and Lyle Vander Broek
and to my sister and her family:
Thelma, Dave, Mark, and Matthew Snyder

Contents

Contents

11 Christian Life 87

12 Reign of God 95

13 Polity 103

For Further Reading 112

Preface

Questions and answers are part of life. We face them every day. They are features of all areas of our existence. We ask; an answer is given. We are asked, and we reply.

So too in Christian faith. A classic definition of theology is that theology is "faith seeking understanding." We believe in the Christian faith and so we are inevitably impelled, by our faith, to seek further understanding—to find answers to our questions. This is the nature of our faith. Christians are never content simply to say, "I believe," and close their minds. We are people of faith who seek further understanding so our knowledge of who God is and what God has done in Jesus Christ can grow. A stagnant faith becomes no faith. A vital faith is one that asks questions and seeks answers.

This is a book of questions and answers. It deals particularly with questions that arise in the context of that stream of Christian theology and belief we call "Presbyterian." I am a Presbyterian. It has been my joy over nearly thirty years as a theologian in the pastorate and in theological education to listen to questions from Presbyterian persons about what Presbyterians believe. Many of these questions are also posed by those in other theological traditions. They are basic to Christian faith itself. But Presbyterians, as vital Christians, seek to enhance their faith by further understanding.

This book is written for laity and students. It tries to give brief answers to these "Presbyterian questions" in a succinct manner. I've written other books that deal in more detail with theological issues of interest to Presbyterians. These are listed in the "For Further Reading" section at the end of this book. I've tried here, however, to begin with the questions that rise in Presbyterian minds that I've heard through the decades, over and over again.

My responses to these questions are intended to open doors to further thought, reflection, discussion, and study. I heard a sermon once entitled "The Peril of the Easy Answer." The theme was that it is often easy to settle for "easy answers" and to avoid more difficult thought—to our peril. I hope my answers here will not be regarded as "easy" because they are brief, or in the sense that they are simplistic. I tried to write here as nontechnically as possible so the responses are accessible to those with little or no previous knowledge of Presbyterian beliefs.

Presbyterians are part of the ecumenical church and the whole wide stream of Christian theology. But we do have a Presbyterian tradition of theology, often called "Reformed theology." I am fully aware of the varieties within the term "Presbyterian theology" and recognize we have a number of denominations today that are called "Presbyterian." At some points I have needed to say some Presbyterians believe this, some believe that on a certain issue. My own denomination is the Presbyterian Church (U.S.A.). This book will find most of its readers within this church family, I am sure. But I hope that Presbyterians in other Presbyterian denominations as well will find it useful and accurate. The book can serve, I trust, as a snapshot of Presbyterian beliefs for anyone in any church who is interested in this subject. I want to open doors to understanding Presbyterian beliefs through theological questions that are part of Christian experience and which Presbyterians ask.

Many more questions could be added to each topic here. The chapters are the traditional doctrines of theology. I have included a chapter on "Presbyterian History and Heritage" as well as one on "Polity" (church government), to say a bit about this aspect of Presbyterian theological practice. I have made a few citations from various confessional documents. For convenience sake, the *Book of Confessions* of the Presbyterian Church (U.S.A.) has been used as the reference source, and abbreviated as *BC* in the text.

I would like to thank those who assisted with this project by providing their questions for consideration in this book. I have benefited from their kindnesses. Good help from former students and friends in churches helped make these "real questions" and not just ones of my own devising.

My gratitude to my wonderful family, LindaJo, Stephen, and Karl McKim, is deep and never-ending. Their love and support make all my labors a joy.

This book is dedicated to our friends Rebecca and Ron Cole-Turner and Rachel and Lyle Vander Broek. Their care and love through the years has been a blessed part of our lives. It is also dedicated to my sister Thelma, her husband, Dave, and sons, Mark and Matthew Snyder, in gratitude for our family love.

Donald K. McKim
Germantown, Tennessee
Epiphany of the Lord
January 6, 2003

Ways to Use This Book

This book can be used in different ways.

Group Study. This book has thirteen chapters, designed so that groups in churches can study one chapter a week through a quarter of the church year. The seven questions for each chapter (except the chapter on the Bible, which has eight) can be read by participants as a question and answer per day through the week. I hope this "easy dose" approach will encourage participants to read each chapter and then discuss it when the group gathers weekly. I imagine each question/answer will evoke further questions or perspectives, which can be discussed by the group as a whole. I hope so! Of course, the time period for the group study can be extended into virtually any format. Church groups such as church sessions, new members classes, Sunday school or adult study groups are contexts in which I trust this book will be helpful.

Individual Study. This book is also designed for individual study. I wrote it for those interested in knowing about Presbyterian beliefs. These may be persons who have a general interest, those who are considering membership in Presbyterian churches, those who are joining Presbyterian churches from other denominations, seminary students, or longtime Presbyterians who would like a focused look at our theological understandings. Individuals can use this book in nearly any way. I hope some will be encouraged to delve further into the many resources available so their Christian faith will be enhanced by greater understanding.

1

Presbyterian History and Heritage

1. Where do Presbyterian churches come from?

Presbyterians are found all over the globe! Each particular Presbyterian congregation has its own history. The Presbyterian churches in a region or a country also have distinctive histories of their own.

Our "family tree" as Presbyterians extends back to Europe in the sixteenth century. We Presbyterians, in our various forms, trace our theological ancestry to the Swiss Reformation. Then, leaders of the newly emerging Protestant faith were witnessing to their Christian faith and were critical of beliefs and practices of the current Roman Catholic Church. The Protestant Reformation that began with Martin Luther (1483–1546) in Germany moved into Switzerland. There, however, other leaders arose who were critical of Roman Catholicism but did not fully agree theologically with Luther. These leaders became known as "Reformed." Major figures were Huldrych Zwingli (1484–1531), John Calvin (1509–64), and Heinrich Bullinger (1504–75). Calvin became the most highly regarded of these leaders.

The beliefs of these theologians spread, and along with their theology a form of governing churches based on the centrality of "presbyteries" emerged. Thus the name "Presbyterian" became descriptive. Presbyterianism spread into Great Britain and then to the New World in the United States and Canada. Those who espoused Presbyterian theology also made their way throughout other countries, until today Presbyterian churches are found through all parts of the world.

Churches in the Presbyterian tradition are marked by similar theological beliefs and by a "presbyterian" form of church government. The theological standards or confessions of faith a Presbyterian denomination adopts in different countries or localities will vary. Presbyterians have always constructed confessions of faith in their various localities. So there is not one, single, "Presbyterian" document that is the official "confession" of Presbyterian churches. Instead, we draw from the resources of a rich tradition. While we look back to our sixteenth-century European roots, we also look forward to further developments in the Presbyterian tradition and to the future to which God calls us.

2. What are the origins of Presbyterian churches in the United States?

Most Presbyterian churches in the United States can trace their ancestry to the waves of European immigrants who came to this country starting in the days of the seventeenth century. A large number of Christians who believed in "Presbyterian theology" emigrated to the United States from Great Britain and the European continent.

Today there are a number of different Presbyterian denominations in the United States. They hold in common a commitment to the "presbyterian" form of church government. They differ in emphases and also, frequently, on the particular confessional standards or confessions of belief they hold as authoritative. The largest Presbyterian denomination, the Presbyterian Church (U.S.A.), has a *Book of Confessions* composed of eleven statements of Christian belief from the early church period to the end of the twentieth century as its standards for theological beliefs. Other Presbyterian denominations often look to the Westminster Confession (1647) as their sole confessional standard.

There have been a number of Presbyterian denominations throughout the history of the United States. These have merged and split from each other, often over particular theological points and sometimes over social practices. The largest Presbyterian bodies in the United States split at the time of the American Civil War (1861–65), primarily over slavery, and did not reunite until 1983. A major issue in the last quarter century has been the ordination of women.

Some current Presbyterian denominations came into existence toward the end of the twentieth century when they rejected the practice of women's ordination engaged in by the largest Presbyterian Church bodies. Earlier theological disputes still linger. There are Presbyterian bodies in the United States today who do not sing hymns, but sing only psalms as found in a Psalter. Presbyterians in the United States have also split into differing bodies over issues of election and predestination, educational standards for clergy, the use of alcohol, and views about the end of the world. While these topics suggest that Presbyterians take theology seriously—which is good—they also bear witness to the fact that the larger "Presbyterian family" is divided within itself, just as Presbyterians are divided from other Christians, and the whole Christian family is also divided among many members. We all need to hear the prayer of Jesus "that they may all be one" (John 17:20–21).

3. What do we mean by a "Reformed" church or "Reformed theology"?

"Reformed" is a term that emerged during the time of the Protestant Reformation in Europe in the sixteenth century. Prior to the Reformation, the Roman Catholic Church and the Eastern Orthodox Church (after 1054) were the major Christian bodies. In 1517, a monk named Martin Luther began a movement that questioned Roman Catholic theology and belief as not being correctly based on the Bible and as incorporating practices that were not biblical. This led to the movement of church reform called the Reformation. "Protestants" were those who were witnessing to the Christian faith as they understood it from the Bible. The movement spread throughout Europe. Luther's followers became known as Lutherans.

Other reformers agreed with Luther's criticisms of the Roman Church, but also began to differ with him on some items of biblical interpretation. This led them to become recognized as another "Protestant" movement. Theologians such as Huldrych Zwingli, John Calvin, and Heinrich Bullinger became leaders of this movement, which became known as the Reformed tradition. The term "Reformed" came from a comment by Queen Elizabeth I in England that the followers of Zwingli and Calvin in England were more "reformed" than the Lutherans, in that they wanted a more thoroughgoing reform of worship practices based on their understanding of the Bible.

"Reformed theology" refers to the theological beliefs taught by these early Reformed theologians and the tradition of their followers that began after their deaths and which continues to the present day. Sometimes Reformed theology is called "Calvinist" theology, and in the tradition of Presbyterian churches is identified as "Presbyterian theology." Reformed theology is marked by a recognition that Christian faith needs constantly to be articulated and confessed. Theologians in the Reformed tradition realize that all our theological statements are, at best, "approximations." We can never absolutize a particular way of speaking Christian truth, because God is always leading us on and giving us new insights from the Scriptures. Yet, Reformed theology seeks to do careful theology so that Reformed churches will have ways of understanding and proclaiming the Christian faith that can speak meaningfully and compellingly to contemporary people in various cultures.

4. What is Calvinism?

Calvinism is associated with the theological understandings of John Calvin. It usually refers to the spread and development of views associated with Calvin from his sixteenth-century context in Geneva throughout the whole of Europe, into the New World, and beyond on to other continents. It is seen as a theological "system," where the different doctrines fit logically together to form a tight, systematic form of Christian theology.

Calvin's followers had a formative and shaping influence as Calvinism spread and developed. Important were Calvin's successor in Geneva, Theodore Beza (1519–1605), and others such as Peter Martyr Vermigli (1500–1562), Girolamo Zanchi (1516–90), and Francis Turretin (1623–87). Significant developing confessional statements were the Scots Confession (1560), the Heidelberg Catechism (1563), the Second Helvetic Confession (1566), and the Westminster Confession of Faith (1647).

The most prominent theological expression of "Calvinism" took shape at the Synod of Dort (1618–19), an assembly of theologians in the Netherlands gathered to settle the predestination controversy between "Calvinists," who followed Calvin, and "Arminians," those who followed Jacob Arminius (1560–1609), a former follower of Calvin who broke with Calvin over views of election and predestination.

The Synod of Dort established five theological points to distinguish Calvinism from Arminianism (and later, by extension, to distinguish Presbyterians from Methodists). The collective first letters of these points spell TULIP, a term appropriate for the Dutch setting.

These are: Total Depravity—that humans are affected by sin in all aspects of life; Unconditional Election—that God elects persons to salvation without foreseeing faith on their part; Limited Atonement—that Christ's death was intended only for the elect; Irresistible Grace—that God's grace in salvation cannot be resisted by humans; and the Perseverance of the Saints—that once Christians are saved, salvation will not be lost.

Historians and theologians disagree on the extent to which all of these together "go beyond" Calvin. Some see the developments as salutary, others do not. But the "five points of Calvinism" have given a specific theological identity. Presbyterians today, in varying degrees, both agree and disagree with the "five points." Some would like to call themselves "Calvinian," instead of "Calvinist" to indicate a closer allegiance to Calvin himself.

5. Why do Presbyterians have so many confessions of faith?

Presbyterians, as part of the Reformed tradition, are people who confess our faith. We create new confessions of faith, since we believe this need to "confess" is inherent in the nature of Christian faith itself. As the psalmist said, "Let the redeemed of the LORD say so" (Ps. 107:2).

God's people have always said what they believe. At significant historical moments, it has been important for the people of God to say who they are and what beliefs they hold most profoundly. These statements of faith become a way of identifying us, and for those who follow in the future a way of passing on the vitality of our deepest faith. This was what the people of Israel did (Deut. 6:4–9; 26:5–9), and the early church used short statements of Christian truth to summarize beliefs (Rom. 10:9; 1 Cor. 12:3; Phil. 2:11).

Presbyterians and other Reformed Christians have a rich heritage of confessions of faith from the period of the Protestant Reformation. Among the most important Reformed statements have been the Scots Confession (1560), the Heidelberg Catechism (1563), the Second Helvetic Confession (1566), and the Westminster Confession of Faith (1647).

In contemporary times, the Theological Declaration of Barmen (1934) was a crucial Christian affirmation in the face of emerging Nazism in Germany. The Confession of 1967 in the United Presbyterian Church in the United States of America applied its central theme of God's reconciliation in Jesus Christ to key social problems of the day. The Presbyterian Church (U.S.A.) adopted "A Brief Statement of Faith" (1993) to summarize contemporary understandings in a document able to be used liturgically in churches.

Presbyterians see confessions of faith as expressing what we believe the Scriptures teach. They are secondary standards to the Bible itself, never to be treated as on a par with Scripture. They are human expressions, always open to revision and reformulation.

They are ways for Presbyterians to express our perspectives as part of the "catholic," or universal, church. We desire to confess our faith as we continue to listen to God's Word. We want to communicate to our contemporaries and to future generations what we hear God's Spirit saying to the churches (Rev. 3:22).

6. What makes Presbyterians different from Lutherans, or Methodists, or Baptists?

There have been historic theological differences between Presbyterians and other Protestant traditions such as the Lutheran, Methodist, and Baptist.

One major divide is that the Presbyterian, Lutheran, and Methodist traditions believe in infant baptism while the various Baptist traditions do not. Baptists believe that only those who are old enough ("adult") to make a profession of their faith in Jesus Christ should be baptized. The infant baptism traditions (including the Roman Catholic tradition) believe baptism should be administered to the children of Christian believers as a sign of their incorporation into the family of Christian faith.

The Presbyterian, Lutheran, and Methodist traditions have different forms of church government (polity). The Lutheran and Methodist traditions have a hierarchical form of polity, with bishops exercising authority in many church matters. Presbyterian polity features elected members of presbyteries as the focus of authority and decision making.

Theologically, Presbyterians and Lutherans have historically held different views about the presence of Christ in the Lord's Supper, the relation of God's law to the gospel, and the nature of faith in baptism.

Presbyterians and Methodists have chiefly been known for disagreements on issues of election and predestination and whether or not humans have "free will." The theological topics of sanctification and Christian "perfection" have also been sources of differences.

Thus, varying approaches to theology and church government

have accounted for many of the historical differences among these denominations. Worship practices also vary. Yet, depending on the place and the particular church, many Presbyterians can feel very much "at home" attending worship in churches of other denominations. Theological conversations are held at various levels among these church bodies. To date, their results have been of interest, but have not made a significant impact on churches either at the denominational or local levels. It is important for Presbyterians to know Presbyterian theology and heritage. This helps us as we dialogue with friends and neighbors of other traditions. Our hope is that this knowledge helps us participate better ecumenically, so that we may be "good stewards of the manifold grace of God" (1 Pet. 4:10).

7. Why are Presbyterians associated with "predestination"?

The doctrine of predestination has long been part of the Presbyterian tradition. It was part of the theology of John Calvin and developed further by Calvin's followers. Predestination, or election, played a role in the important theological disputes in the seventeenth century between the Calvinists and the Arminians. In America, these disagreements translated into differences between Presbyterians and Methodists on the doctrine.

Predestination is part of the biblical and Christian tradition. It was given prominence by the theologian Augustine (354–430). Calvin and his later followers were highly influenced by Augustine's understandings of the doctrine and developed it further in their own sixteenth and seventeenth-century contexts. Thus, predestination became associated with Presbyterians.

Often the doctrine of election, or predestination, is caricatured. It is said to be a harsh doctrine, turning God into a tyrant. Or it is said to deny that humans can make any choices because "everything is predestined." Another way predestination is sometimes described is to say it is just a theological word for "fate."

To the Presbyterian, none of these are correct understandings.

Calvin came to the doctrine from a very pastoral concern: Why is it some people respond to the Christian gospel and others do not? His answer, as he studied Scripture, was that God had elected or chosen ("predestined," as Rom. 8:28–30) those who believe. This is a gift of God's grace, because humans are sinners and do not deserve the salvation God gives as a free gift in Jesus Christ. For Calvin, predestination should lead to gratitude and joy! It means that when we believe the gospel, we believe because of God's powerful Spirit in our lives, and that God has elected us out of God's free grace.

When Presbyterians talk about predestination, we are talking about the actions of the God of the Bible. God is not the blind laws of nature or an impersonal force (like "fate"). God here chooses to enter into relationships with sinful people (covenants) and to provide the gift of salvation by sending Jesus Christ into the world (John 3:16–21). This is a God who cares and loves and gives grace to undeserving people like us. So predestination is a comforting doctrine, since it assures us that our salvation rests in God's work, not our own.

Predestination is not the only thing Presbyterians believe! But we can be grateful for our understandings of predestination, not because they show us as worthy of God's love, but because we experience the loving power of God, who "proves his love for us in that while we still were sinners Christ died for us" (Rom. 5:8). This is the joy of predestination!

2

Bible

8. What is the basic message of the Bible?

Some see the Bible to be a drama in three acts: Creation, Fall, and Redemption. Another way to put this is to say that the message of the Bible is:

> God created the world good.
> Humans messed up the good creation.
> God came in Jesus Christ to set things right.

The richness and the fullness of what the Bible communicates is much more detailed and richer than these three "basics." But, broadly speaking, the whole of Scripture is encompassed by these three points.

God created the world good. This is vital and is the Bible's first statement (Gen. 1:1–2). We know who we are and where all things originated. We are God's children. All things come from God. God's verdict on the creation was: "and indeed, it was very good" (Gen. 1:31). God the Creator is a constant theme in Scripture. The greatness and goodness of God lead humans to praise the creator of all things (Pss. 103, 104), including us! (Ps. 8).

Humans messed up the good creation. The story of sin (Gen. 3) is of humans who have chosen to live according to our own wills and agendas, rather than seeking the purposes and directions that our Creator intends. We have broken God's laws and, even more, broken God's heart because we have rejected the relationship of love God wants to have with each of us. God's "steadfast love" which pervades the earth (Ps. 33:5) has been rejected by unfaithful people.

God came in Jesus Christ to set things right. This is the gospel, the "good news"! Our relationships with God—broken by sin—are now restored and made new through our Lord and Savior Jesus Christ. God loved the world so much that God sent the Son of God into the world to provide the means, through his death and resurrection, of bringing new, "eternal" life to sinners (John 3:16–17). This is the greatest news we can ever hear! It is the message Presbyterians share vigorously with the whole world. Through Christ, "all things, whether on earth or in heaven" will be reconciled to God, since God in Christ is "making peace through the blood of his cross" (Col. 1:20).

9. What is the purpose of the Bible?

The Westminster Shorter Catechism, an important Presbyterian catechism from the seventeenth century, asks: "What do the Scriptures principally teach?" The answer: "The Scriptures principally teach what man is to believe concerning God, and what duty God requires of man" (*BC* 7.003). This is the Bible's purpose: to teach us what to believe and how to live.

We see these foci in two biblical verses, one each from the New and Old Testaments. The Gospel of John concludes by saying that Jesus did many other signs "which are not written in this book." But, "these are written so that you may come to believe that Jesus is the Messiah, the Son of God, and that through believing you may have life in his name" (John 20:31). The church has seen this purpose as extending to the Bible as a whole. Here, as nowhere else, we find the witness of faith to Jesus as God's Son, the Messiah. Through the Scriptures, we come to believe in Jesus Christ and to have the "life" God intends us to have, through him. This, we believe.

The second verse is a high point of Old Testament ethics. The prophet Micah proclaims what God requires: "He has told you, O mortal, what is good; and what does the LORD require of you but to do justice, and to love kindness, and to walk humbly with your God?" (Mic. 6:8). This is the duty and purpose for living of those created by God. We are to uphold what is right in accord with God's will, act in ways that convey the mercy and faithfulness of God, and thus to live in humble obedience and fellowship with the Lord. This, God desires.

Presbyterians see the Bible as our source for the unique knowledge and understandings indicated here. The Bible is our way of knowing what to believe about God and supremely what God has done in Jesus Christ. We learn this nowhere else than in the Scriptures. Sometimes the term "infallible" is used to designate this conviction that the Bible will not lead us astray in what to believe. Here also we find how God wants us to live. God's law is revealed to show us God's will. As Christians, we obey God's law out of gratitude for God's love. Put simply: the one who loves "has fulfilled the law" (Rom. 13:8). So the Bible is the incomparable basis to enable our beliefs and our actions to be united.

10. What do we mean when we say the Bible is "God's Word"?

Presbyterians affirm that the Bible is God's Word because we believe that the Scriptures of the Old and New Testaments are God's self-revelation. Through the Bible we gain a knowledge of God that is unique and authoritative for the church and for Christian life. We call the Bible "God's Word" as a way of affirming this book is a special and distinctive source for our knowledge of God.

"God's Word" means God's self-expression. We are familiar with the important verse that begins the Gospel of John: "In the beginning was the Word, and the Word was with God, and the Word was God" (John 1:1). This verse points to Jesus Christ as the "Word" of God, the one who has become "flesh and lived among us" (John 1:14). So Jesus Christ is the primary expression of God, the "self-revelation" of God.

But we learn of Jesus Christ through the Scriptures. The church has believed through the centuries that the Bible is also properly called the "Word of God" because it is the source of our knowledge of Jesus Christ and of our knowledge of God's actions in the history of Israel. The books of the Old and New Testaments, the "canon," are regarded as the place where God's word is heard as God spoke and acted in Israel's history as we find in the Old Testament, in the person of Jesus Christ, and in the life of the early church as found in the writings of the New Testament.

So the Bible is called the Word of God because in Scripture the church is addressed by the God who inspired the biblical writings. The Scriptures of the Old and New Testaments are God's self-revelation and the means by which God continues to speak to us today.

11. Why is the Bible considered an authority for the church?

We frequently notice on the cover of a Bible the phrase "Holy Bible." The term "holy" means two things. "Holy" means "pure" or "sacred." It also means "set apart" or "unique." The Bible is unique or set apart from other books, so it is called "holy."

The reason the Bible is regarded as an authority for the church is that the church believes the Bible is special. It is a unique book because it is the source through which God's self-communication or "revelation" is conveyed. God's revelation means God's "uncovering" or "making known" of something. The church has believed that in the Bible God makes known who God is and what God has done. In the Bible, God's actions in history have been recorded from the perspective of those who have faith. The writers in the Hebrew Bible (the Old Testament) perceived God's acts in history in the nation of Israel. The writers of the New Testament believed God was uniquely and definitively revealed in the person of Jesus of Nazareth. The collection of biblical books, called the "canon," is the set of writings the church views as the source of its knowledge of God.

Why does the church make this claim that the Bible is an authority? Part of the church's view, in addition to the conviction that

God is revealed in the Bible, is that Scripture is inspired by God. That is, God is the one who "stands behind" the biblical writings. Those who wrote the Scriptures wrote as people who lived in their own times and places, their own historical contexts. But the church also believes that God was especially active in the recording and transmission of the Scripture in "inspiration." There is an interplay between God's divine inspiration and the expression of God's message through the biblical writers in their own words. So while we read these ancient documents as writings by persons who lived completely in their own social settings, we also read these documents as being expressions of God's message to these biblical writers. How inspiration occurred is a mystery. But the church's confession is that the Bible is an authority for the church's life because it is God's self-revelation expressed through God's special inspiration of those who wrote and of what they wrote.

12. Since we have the New Testament, why do we need the Old Testament?

Presbyterians, with other Christians, affirm that both the Hebrew Scriptures (Old Testament) and the New Testament are the Word of God and are essential for the church's life and belief. Early in its history, the church rejected the views of those like Marcion who argued that the Old Testament was not necessary for Christian understanding.

Both testaments are vital to understanding who God is and what God has done. The Old Testament is the witness to Israel's faith in the God who liberated the people from Egypt, called them into covenantal relationship, and gave them the Law as a guide for doing God's will. This God of Israel had made a covenant with Abraham and Sarah to be the God of their descendants and to make them numerous (Gen. 17). God's covenant promises were affirmed in other places, with other persons, such as David, to whom God promised a dynasty (2 Sam. 7:1–17; 23:5; Ps. 89:3) and what later became the "messianic hope" of the prophets (Isa. 11:1–9). God will send a promised "Messiah" to be God's "anointed one" (the meaning of the term), who as king will perfectly represent God and establish God's reign at the end of time (Jer. 23:5–6; Zech. 9:9–10).

So the Old Testament with all its narratives and rich teaching is the context out of which Jesus emerged. Followers of Jesus believe that he is the promised Messiah, from the line of David, and that he in himself fulfills the promises made by God in the various covenants of the Hebrew Scriptures. The word "testament" comes from the Latin term *testamentum,* which means "covenant." So to say the "Old Testament" is also to say the "Old Covenant."

Theologically, the Old Testament provides the "promise," the New Testament the "fulfillment" (Heb. 6:13–20). Thus there is an important relationship between the two testaments. One cannot be fully understood without the other. Presbyterian Christians have maintained that the "substance" of the Old Covenant and the New Covenant are the same, but God's covenant relationship with the people of God has been expressed differently in different periods. The final and definitive expression of this covenant relationship is in Jesus Christ, who is the "new covenant," the fulfillment of God's promises (Jer. 31:31–34; 1 Cor. 11:23–26).

13. Are there errors in the Bible?

This question usually assumes that what we mean by "errors" are such things as the mistakes we might find today in reading a book on history or science. "Error" is that which is not consistent with what we know by different means of verification—such as by the laws of logic, or the testimony of eyewitnesses, or established laws of science. This definition of error is very clear-cut.

Some Christians believe the Bible cannot properly be called the "Word of God" if it could be proved that even one historical or scientific error is found within its pages. If God is perfect, they argue, then God's "Word" must also be perfect—a single error casts doubt on the truth of God. A refinement is to say that there can be no such "errors" in the original biblical writings (*auto-*

grapha). This qualification is necessary because the Bible as we have it now is a synthesis of a number of manuscripts or copies of texts. So it is possible that some scribe could have made an error in copying a word, and an "error" could creep into a biblical text. Some Presbyterians have held to this theory, called "biblical inerrancy."

Yet this is not the only way to view this question. Other Presbyterians, who are equally committed to affirming the Bible's authority, believe that this understanding of "error" is not an appropriate way to approach the Bible. The Scriptures are ancient documents, written by people who were not concerned with the same kinds of issues of "science" or "history" that we are today. We should not expect the same standards for "accuracy" from them if this was not their goal. Biblically, one is in "error" when one deviates or goes "astray" from God's truth as an expression of God's will (1 Cor. 12:2; Titus 3:3; 1 Pet. 2:25). This is "error" of the most serious kind. No Presbyterian believes this kind of "error" is in the Bible. The Bible is trustworthy and reliable as the source for our knowledge of God and how God wants us to live—in this sense the Bible is "infallible." Even if there were historical or scientific errors in the Bible, this would not diminish what the Bible is: God's divinely revealed source for knowing who God is and what God has done, especially in giving us salvation in Jesus Christ.

So the answer to our question relates to how we define "error." It also relates to our view of the nature of Scripture and how God works through the Bible to be revealed to us.

14. How do Presbyterians interpret the Bible?

Presbyterians take biblical interpretation very seriously. We believe that the Scriptures are God's Word and that we should use the best resources we have available to help us hear and understand what God is saying through the biblical texts.

A 1982 study, elaborated on in 1983, has given the Presbyterian

Church (U.S.A.) a helpful set of guidelines for interpreting the Bible.* These should be taken together, so that we can adopt an approach to biblical interpretation that maintains fidelity to God's Word.

1. *Recognize that Jesus Christ, the Redeemer, Is the Center of Scripture.* Luther called the Bible "the cradle in which Christ lies." The Old Testament anticipates Christ; the New Testament witnesses to his coming as God's Messiah who has redeemed his people. Jesus Christ is the central focus of the biblical story.

2. *Focus on the Plain Text of Scripture.* Some biblical texts are clearly symbolic, many others are best understood when we know the particular settings and customs of the time. We need to know as much as we can about the biblical languages and the social and cultural contexts of the biblical writings to interpret them well and take the Bible seriously.

3. *Depend on the Holy Spirit's Guidance for Interpreting and Applying God's Message.* The Holy Spirit enables us to see and hear things in the biblical texts that may have been hidden to us before. God's Word and God's Spirit always go together. Prayer for the Spirit's illumination is always important for biblical interpretation and for applying the Bible's word.

4. *Be Guided by the Church's Doctrinal Consensus or "Rule of Faith."* The church has interpreted the Bible through the centuries. We should always pay attention to what the church has heard the Spirit saying in Scripture, and recognize as significant the creeds and confessions of the ancient church as well as of other Reformed churches when we interpret.

5. *Let All Interpretations Be in Accord with the "Rule of Love."* Jesus commanded us to love God and love our neighbor. Later theologians spoke of the "rule of love" as being a guide for us, in that our biblical interpretation should not lead us toward views or

---

* I have slightly modified the points in the two reports for brevity here. The reports are available together from the Presbyterian Church (U.S.A.) as *Presbyterian Understanding and Use of Holy Scripture* and *Biblical Authority and Interpretation* (Louisville, Ky.: Office of the General Assembly, 1992). Address: 100 Witherspoon St., Louisville, KY 40202–1396. Online see www.pcusa.org/marketplace.The documents can be ordered through "The Presbyterian Marketplace" section and are item number OGA 99022.

actions that are destructive of or harmful to others, since we are clearly commanded to love them.

6. *Remember That Biblical Interpretation Requires Earnest Study.* No amount of prayer or piety is a substitute for using the best resources available to us for helping with biblical interpretation. Today we have many such aids, a large number written for those with no specific theological training. These should be appropriated and well used.

7. *Seek to Interpret a Particular Biblical Passage in Light of All of the Bible.* Biblical interpretation should move from "the whole to the part." The big, overarching messages of Scripture should help us understand particular biblical passages. They should also stand as guides to warn us if our individual interpretations are moving in directions contrary to the larger, clearer biblical themes.

These guidelines do not "ensure" that our biblical interpretation will automatically be best. But they do orient us toward a Presbyterian perspective on Scripture that can open us to hearing "what the Spirit is saying to the churches" (Rev. 2:7).

15. Do Presbyterians believe in a literal Adam and Eve?

Some do and some don't! For many centuries, nearly all Christians believed that the Adam and Eve whose story is told in the opening chapters of the book of Genesis were real, historical persons.

Things changed, however, as biblical scholars, particularly since the eighteenth century, began to understand more clearly the nature of the biblical writings. "Biblical criticism" is a term used, not to denote "criticism" of the Bible in the sense of disparaging it or being "critical" of the Scriptures, but rather as a way of evaluating Scripture. Biblical criticism since the eighteenth century has begun to recognize that the Bible has a number of different types of literature in it—not all of which is intended to be interpreted historically or literally. This is true to a large degree with the literature in the Psalms, which is highly poetic in nature, as well as for the parables of Jesus. Jesus' parables do not depend on whether or not they are literally or historically true in order for them to convey important truths to us.

Similarly, biblical scholars have helped us recognize that the early chapters of Genesis are stories that circulated throughout the history of Israel, written to explain the origin of the world and all things, including humans. The truth of what the stories are trying to convey is a theological truth. It does not necessarily have to be a historical truth. The theological purposes of the stories are to provide a way of understanding who humans are, that the world and all things originated from God, and that all the created order stands in a relationship with the Creator. These truths are valid whether or not the events of the early Genesis chapters are interpreted in a literal way.

So, while some Presbyterians may believe that Adam and Eve were real, historical persons, other Presbyterians do not. Yet, in both cases, the truths that the stories in Genesis were written to convey can be realized and believed.

3

God

16. Can we prove that God exists?

Some philosophers and theologians through the centuries have developed formal, logical arguments to "prove" that God exists. Five of these have had particular importance. They are the ontological, teleological, cosmological, causal, and moral. These were given particular prominence by the medieval theologian Thomas Aquinas (1225–74). They have been used through the years both to try to persuade people to believe in God on the basis of rational, intellectual arguments and also to assure those who already believe in God that their belief is not irrational or merely a matter of feeling, habit, or social conformity.

The logical validity of these "theistic proofs," as they are sometimes called, has been challenged through the years as well. Some believe that the arguments cannot stand up to logical scrutiny and that they do not rationally "prove" that a God exists.

The approach of the Bible is far different. The Bible does not try to prove God's existence; it assumes it. The first verse of the Bible says, "In the beginning when God created the heavens and the earth . . . " (Gen. 1:1). No matter whether the logical arguments are valid or not, they cannot tell us the nature of the "God" they may prove. They cannot tell us what God must be like.

But this is the intention of the Bible. The question that matters most for humans is not simply whether God exists but, if God does exist, what is this God's nature? Is God merely a "force" (as in "May the force be with you") or is God personal? If God is personal, then is God a tyrant, wicked, good, loving? The questions throng.

The debate about the proofs should alert us to what is really crucial for us: to know who God is and what God is like. Beyond the "logical proofs," there is the "proof" of Christian experience. We know God by our experience of God—through the Scriptures, the church, and in our own lives. The personal God we know in this way—the God of the Bible—is the God with whom we have to deal in life and death. Our personal faith in this God produces the strongest "proof" of the reality of God. As Pascal the philosopher put it, "The heart has its reasons which reason does not know."

17. How can we know God?

There is really only one way to know God: that is, if God chooses to become known.

We all recognize the great difference between God and humans. In the language of philosophy and theology, God is "transcendent"—over and beyond us, and infinite. Humans are limited and finite. We are humans; God is God.

This great gulf between us and God can never be bridged by human actions. We cannot storm the gates of heaven, pull back the clouds, and peer into God's face! We are on earth; God is in heaven. As God said to Isaiah, "My thoughts are not your thoughts, nor are your ways my ways" (Isa. 55:8). Limited human beings cannot meet God on "equal terms."

So, if we are ever to know anything about God or to "know God," it must be God who takes the initiative to become known. God must be the one to "make the first move."

Astoundingly, we Presbyterians, along with other Christians, believe God has done this! God has communicated God's own self to us. Theologically, this self-communication is God's "revelation." That which is hidden has been made known. The God who is greater than us in every way has chosen to communicate with humanity and to impart knowledge of who God is. Even more astonishingly, we can "know" God in the way that we say we "know" other people.

God's revelation comes in two forms. "General revelation" is the knowledge of God gathered from nature around us, or from our human minds. If we look at a sunset, we might reason that there must be a "God" behind it all. This is sometimes called "natural revelation."

Yet, any kind of knowledge gained through nature or our own minds is not enough. Even if it convinces us that there is a God, it does not tell us what this God is like. Even more, sin causes humans to reject and "suppress" this knowledge gained from the visible world (Rom. 1:18-23). More is needed. So Christians believe in God's "special revelation." God is revealed to us in the Scriptures and, supremely, in Jesus Christ, the focus of God's special revelation. He is "Emmanuel"—"God is with us." Nature or human reasoning can never reveal that! Only God can. To know God by faith this way is to look at God's "general revelation" with new eyes. Now nature around us can be seen as the theater of God's glory, and now to us "the heavens are telling the glory of God; and the firmament proclaims his handiwork" (Ps. 19:1).

18. What is the Trinity?

The Trinity is a term used to express the Christian church's belief that the eternal God in whom we believe is "one God in three persons." While this is a rather simple statement, the doctrine of the Trinity is very complex and is ultimately a mystery.

Early Christians worshiped the God who had been revealed to the nation of Israel in the Old Testament. This is the God who liberated the people from Egypt in the exodus (Ex. 20:2). This is the God to whom Jesus prayed (John 17).

But early Christians also believed that in the person of Jesus of Nazareth they encountered God in an altogether unique way. In the early centuries of the Christian church, the church confessed its belief that Jesus Christ was also God.

Relatedly, earliest Christians after the day of Pentecost (Acts 2) believed that God was present in the church and in their experience in the Holy Spirit. The Spirit also is God, just as is Jesus Christ, and the God who created the heavens and the earth (Gen. 1), the God of Israel.

In the fourth century, the church wrote the Nicene Creed to express the conviction that the God it worships is Father, Son, and Holy Spirit. These are three "persons" who are at the same time one "God." They are eternal and share the same "substance" or "essence" or reality. They are "God" in a way altogether different than us who are "humans." These three persons exist eternally in the Godhead. They "indwell" each other, meaning that they share a divine life in a dynamic relationship that we characterize as a relationship of love (1 John 4:8, 16). The God of whom we read in the Scriptures is the God who exists eternally and who has acted in history, entering into a relationship with the nation of Israel in the Old Testament, being revealed in the person of Jesus Christ, and continuing to be present with the church through the Holy Spirit. Father, Son, and Holy Spirit are the "three persons" of the Trinity, who in their relationship with each other are also "one God."

19. What are some practical results of believing in the Trinity?

Belief in the Trinity, that God is "one God in three persons" as Father, Son, and Holy Spirit, is a mysterious teaching and one that may seem far removed from everyday life. But it is a basic doctrine and one that Presbyterians share with all other Christians. Belief in the Trinity also leads to some very practical results.

For one thing, the Trinity shows us something about social relationships. The church believes that all three persons of the Trinity are God and that all are equal in power and glory. One of the views that the early church rejected was called "subordinationism." This was the view that Jesus was subordinate to God the Father in a way that meant he was "less" than God. Instead, the church affirmed in

its early creeds that all three members of the Trinity shared "God-
ness" equally (they are of the same substance; the Greek term used
was *homoousios*).

If so, and if the three persons of the Trinity exist in a divine
equality, we can believe also that this is the pattern God wants
humans to follow in their relationships with others. We regard all
persons equally, not with a "hierarchical" attitude that some are
"better" than others, but with "equality." So racism, sexism,
ageism, and all other stereotypes are contrary to the model of the
Trinity.

A second practical result of believing in the Trinity is that the
Trinity shows us that our lives are meant to be relational. We speak
of the three "persons" of the Trinity. Today we tend to think of
"persons" as individuals, as being self-sufficient, and as existing in
and of themselves. When the church described the Trinity as comprised of three persons, it was recognizing that there is a divine
interrelationship among the three. The term "indwelling" (Gr.,
periochoresis) was used to indicate that the members of the Trinity shared a thorough participation with each other, a "circulating
of the divine life," so to speak.

If the Trinity is a model or pattern for us, we realize that we are
created to share our human lives with one another, to participate in
the lives of others, and to see ourselves not as isolated units or
"individuals," but as those created for relationships with our fellow human beings. These relationships should be marked by the
love that exists within the Godhead (John 14:31; 1 John 3:1).

20. What is the providence of God?

God's providence refers to God's interaction with the world.
The term comes from the Latin word *providere* meaning "to provide for" or "to foresee." Theologically, providence is often said
to be comprised of God's preserving creation, cooperating with all
creatures, and guiding or governing all things toward the accom-
plishment of God's purposes.

When Presbyterians affirm that God creates all things (Gen. 1), we realize that we need to take another step. If God created all and then stepped away from the creation, everything would collapse. For the creation to continue, there is need for God to preserve and sustain what is created. The Scriptures affirm that God, out of love, continues to care for creation and to be involved in it, so that all things created can continue in their created state.

This caring love expresses itself in God's desire to interact with the creation, particularly with us as humans. That is, God relates to us, is involved with us, and helps us as we live our lives. God is not a "remote creator." God is concerned with the creation and with each person. Our actions matter to God. God providentially cooperates with us so that we can pray to God, listen for God's word to us, and trust God's love to be at work for our good (Rom. 8:28).

In the bigger picture, God also governs or guides the world to accomplish the purposes that God has determined. God is moving all creation toward a final goal or purpose: the establishment of God's reign in "a new heaven and a new earth" (Rev. 21:1–2). God has a purpose or plan for the whole creation and also for each human life. God is at work in history to accomplish this divine plan (Eph. 1:10; 3:9). God is at work within our lives to carry out the purposes God has for us as individuals (Pss. 57:2; 138:8; Prov. 16:4).

So God's providence is at work both generally, in relation to the whole of creation, and also specially, in relation to our own personal lives.

21. Does God will evil and suffering in the world and in our lives?

No. Presbyterians, with other Christians, do not believe that God wills evil or that God desires suffering in our lives.

God is good (Ps. 73:1), and all that God creates is good (Gen. 1:31; 1 Tim. 4:4). Evil is what opposes God and goes against God's purposes. We speak of "natural evil" as those things occurring in nature which bring devastation, tragedy, or loss of life. We speak of an "evil empire" or an "evil person" to say we perceive that groups of people or individuals can stand in opposition to God and what God wants for the world and human life. Most clearly, we know what God's purposes are when we look at Jesus Christ, who is the "image of the invisible God" (Col. 1:15). When powers or forces are in opposition to God in Christ, they may be called "antichrist" (1 John 2:22; 4:3). Jesus sought to overcome evil by doing good (Acts 10:38).

So we do not speak of God willing evil or suffering in the world. Evil may occur when persons use their powers of choice to choose to do things that are contrary to God's will and purposes. God does not override our freedom to make choices that result in evil. But Presbyterians believe that God can bring good out of evil, and that even as people choose to do evil, God can use it for good (Gen. 50:20; Rom. 8:28), and that human evil cannot thwart God's ultimate plans for us and for creation. The clearest example of this is in the evil done to Jesus in his crucifixion. God conquered this evil in Jesus' resurrection.

When we have evil done against us, or when we suffer for no apparent reason, our response is to trust that God will be present with us. We do not know reasons for evil or suffering. What we do believe by faith is that God will be with us in the midst of our sufferings and that God's grace and power of love will enable us to endure, even in the "darkest valley" (Ps. 23:4). So we are sustained. We believe God can use the evil and suffering we encounter and do within us "far more than all we can ask or imagine" (Eph. 3:20). This is our comfort and our hope.

22. Is God male?

No. But it is easy to get that impression when we listen to the church's language about God through the years. In particular, church references to the deity very often refer to God as "he." Jesus referred to God as "Father" (Matt. 6:9), and the Holy Spirit is often called "he" as well. With Jesus, the whole Trinity is often designated with the male pronoun.

Languages other than English may not have the same difficulties as we do with these kinds of issues. But in English-speaking countries, using the translations of the English Bible that have come down to us, Presbyterian churches—with other Christian communions—have historically used male-oriented language for God in prayers, preaching, and other theological expressions of faith. Thus, it is easy to get the impression that God is male.

The past forty years in Western cultures have brought the awareness of this problem to the forefront. Women in churches had heard God referred to almost exclusively in male terms. But feminist biblical scholars and theologians have helped churches recognize that our traditional theological language has slipped easily into these patterns, whereas biblical imagery for God is much wider and more inclusive than has often been recognized. This is now reflected in "A Brief Statement of Faith" (1993) of the Presbyterian Church (U.S.A.), which includes both gender images for God in the confession:

> Like a mother who will not forsake her nursing child,
> like a father who runs to welcome the prodigal home,
>   God is faithful still.
>
> <div align="right">(<i>BC</i> 10.3, lines 49–51)</div>

Biblical allusions here include Isaiah 49:14–15; 66:13; Luke 13:34–35, as well as Luke 15:11–32.

This is important because, theologically, God is not male or female. "God is spirit," said Jesus (John 4:24). "I am God and no mortal, the Holy One in your midst," said God to the prophet Hosea (Hos. 11:9). None of our English pronouns—or nouns!—can ever say all there is to say about God, or capture the essence of the biblical God. So our language about God needs to reflect the fullness of the biblical witness and to affirm what Elihu said to Job: "God is greater than any mortal" (Job 33:12)—in every way.

4

Jesus Christ

23. What is the incarnation?

The incarnation is a theological term to affirm that Jesus Christ, the second person of the Trinity, became a human being in the person of Jesus of Nazareth. This is a central element of Christian belief and is captured in John's Gospel: "And the Word became flesh and lived among us" (John 1:14). This is "eternity" entering "time," but more importantly it is the ultimate expression of God's love for the humanity created by God and reconciled back to God by the sending of God's Son into the world to bring salvation (John 3:16–17).

Presbyterians affirm that the incarnation took place in the person of Jesus of Nazareth, a Palestinian Jew who was a truly human person as well as being truly and fully divine. This is sometimes called the "paradox" of the incarnation—that Jesus is both fully divine and fully human. Yet this has been the crucial affirmation of the church about Christology, or the study of Christ: Jesus is the "divine-human." Both aspects are critical in our saying who Jesus is.

How Jesus could be truly human and truly divine at the same time is a mystery. It defies rational explanation or confirmation. We affirm it by faith, believing that Jesus took upon himself the sin of humanity, representing us and dying for us. His death has the power to bring salvation because Jesus Christ is fully God. Only one who is fully God and fully human could provide salvation by dying for our sin and being raised in his resurrection.

The church has long affirmed that the two natures of Christ—divine and human—are united in the one person of Jesus Christ. Some groups have emphasized one dimension over the other—the divine over the human, or vice versa. All these attempts have been rejected by the church as being less than a full incarnation—a full affirmation that in Jesus Christ, God has become a human and has assumed human "flesh." Through the experience of redemption and salvation we come to recognize who Jesus is and to realize the importance of what Jesus has done.

In Jesus Christ, God's "power is made perfect in weakness" (2 Cor. 12:9), and salvation is given to those who believe (1 Pet. 1:9). In him, the power of God's love is able to transform the world and to transform human lives. This is our joy in believing in the incarnation of Jesus Christ.

24. Where was Jesus before he came to earth?

Presbyterians affirm the Christian belief in the Trinity. The eternal God is Father, Son, and Holy Spirit. The three persons are one God and share fully in the divine life as "God."

This means that Jesus Christ, the second person of the Trinity, has always existed. He is the eternal God, sharing the fullness of divinity with the Father and the Holy Spirit. The early church affirmed this belief quite clearly in distinction from views (such as held by the Arians) that the Son, Jesus Christ, was a creature, the first creature created by God. If so, Jesus would not be eternal, but rather created. There is all the difference in the world—and more!—between saying that Jesus Christ is the "eternal Son of God" and saying that he is the "Son of the eternal God." The first formulation indicates Jesus existed in heaven with God the Father and the Holy Spirit before his birth on earth; the second that he is a creature like all other created beings.

Relatedly, Presbyterians affirm with other Christians Jesus' "preexistence." This expresses our belief in Jesus as the second person of the Trinity, the eternal Son of God. This is most clearly conveyed in the first verse of the Gospel of John: "In the beginning was the Word, and the Word was with God, and the Word was God" (John 1:1; see also Phil. 2:5–8). The preexistence of Jesus Christ is a way to indicate our belief in Jesus' divinity. In him, the reality of God is found, and this has always been the case, eternally. It will always be the case, eternally. When Jesus was sent into the world by God the Father, in the incarnation, he became a human being and lived within the limits of time and space. He died on the cross to bring salvation. To affirm Jesus' preexistence is to confess our belief that Jesus was "fully God" and that what he accomplished for human salvation was done by the power of God and with the divine sanction and authority of the eternal God.

25. Do Presbyterians believe in the virgin birth of Jesus?

The virgin birth of Jesus has long been a contested question. This is so for a number of reasons. Some contemporary persons find it difficult to affirm because it appears to violate our views of human biology. Others believe it is a biblical symbol and not historical fact.

The "virgin birth of Jesus" means most basically that Jesus was conceived apart from a human father. Mary, the mother of Jesus, was a virgin at the time of Jesus' birth (Matt 1:23; Luke 1:27, 34; John 1:13). The doctrine is affirmed in the Apostles' Creed ("born of the virgin Mary") and arose early in the church as a way of asserting that Jesus Christ as God's incarnate Word was genuinely "made flesh" (incarnated) in the person of Jesus of Nazareth. In this respect, it is also an affirmation of the divinity of Jesus Christ.

Scholars indicate there are biblical reasons for believing in the virgin birth and biblical considerations that would question it. The infancy accounts in Matthew and Luke are the most solid evidence for the virgin birth. On the other hand, it is never mentioned by Paul.

Theologically, some have said that if Jesus is fully human, as the church affirms, we should believe that he was born in the same manner as all other humans who have ever lived. In this view, a virgin birth diminishes the full humanity of Christ. Others claim it makes Jesus an odd mixture of "human" and "divine."

Yet other theologians have seen the virgin birth as a historical fact that testifies powerfully to God's marvelous grace. It shows our salvation in Jesus Christ originates with God, just as it ends with God as well. The theologian Karl Barth said the virgin birth marks off the origin of Jesus Christ from the human race, just as his resurrection marks off the end.

One can find Presbyterians who affirm the virgin birth as a historical fact and others who see it as a symbol and believe it is not to be believed in a literal way. Clearly, belief in this doctrine is not essential for salvation, since it is not a key part of the New Testament's witness to Christ. It is a sign, communicating the mystery of God's love coming into the world in Jesus Christ, who suffered and secured our salvation.

26. Why did Jesus come into the world?

There have been a variety of answers in the history of the Christian church to the question of why Jesus came into the world. Put more formally, the question would be: What is the purpose of the incarnation? We can find a number of major themes that have emerged:

Jesus came to illuminate us. Humans live in the darkness of sin, in ignorance, error, and bondage. Jesus came as the "light of the world" (John 8:12), to enlighten us and show us God's ways (John 1:1–9).

Jesus came to restore us. Humans are separated from God by sinful disobedience. Jesus came as a "second Adam," to bring humanity back to God (Rom. 5:14–17) by bringing new life through his obedience.

Jesus came to satisfy God. Humans stand guilty before God, having broken God's laws and rejecting God's law (Rom. 3:23; Luke 15:11–24). Jesus came to obey God's law, and by his sacrifice our guilt is removed.

Jesus came to bring victory. Humans are captive to the power of evil. In his death he became our ransom (Mark 10:45), and in his resurrection Jesus is victorious over powers of sin and death (1 Cor. 15:24–28). Humanity is rescued, and we are saved.

Jesus came to unite us with God. In our sin, we are separated from God. Jesus came to bring us into union with God. We grow in our union until death, when we attain divinization (Rom. 8:11; 2 Pet. 1:4).

Jesus came to justify us. Our pride has produced a sinful nature, which separates us from God's holy righteousness. Jesus came to justify, or set us right with God, by offering himself as the mediator, so by faith we receive his righteousness in place of our own unrighteousness (Eph. 2:4–10).

These views complement each other, providing lenses through which we can understand the purposes of Jesus' coming. Presbyterians can affirm all these different biblical aspects and marvel at the "immeasurable greatness of his power for us who believe" (Eph. 1:19).

27. Why did Jesus have to die?

Jesus died so the Scriptures would be fulfilled (Matt. 26:53–56). But he also had chosen to die as he "set his face to go to Jerusalem" (Luke 9:51), knowing throughout his ministry that suffering lay ahead (Matt. 17:2; Luke 22:15). While Jesus is said to have been handed over to his enemies "according to the definite plan and foreknowledge of God" (Acts 2:23), he asserted of his life: "I lay it down of my own accord. I have power to lay it down, and I have power to take it up again" (John 10:18). Jesus saw his suffering and death as giving his life as "a ransom for many" (Mark 10:45). Thus, we have the sense that God sent Jesus into the world to die to bring salvation (John 3:16–17; Rom. 5:8; Eph. 2:11–22), and that this was a mission that Jesus, as the eternal Son of God, willingly accepted and fulfilled.

Why, then, did Jesus have to die?

Presbyterians affirm theologically that Jesus died as the substitute for sinful humanity, offering himself in his death as the deepest possible expression of God's love, and bearing in himself the sins of the whole world (Isa. 51:5–6; 1 John 2:2). The way in which the cross of Christ redeems, saves, and reconciles has been variously understood. But Jesus' death is his sacrifice, offered in love, for the sin of humanity. He bore our sin (Isa. 53:12; 1 Pet. 2:24) to make us righteous in God's sight (2 Cor. 5:21). Christ redeemed us from the curse of having broken God's law (Gal. 3:13) and died for us—unrighteous sinners that we are—in order to bring us to God (1 Pet. 3:18). Martin Luther spoke of a "happy exchange," in which Christ's righteousness is given to us while our sin is laid on him.

The death of Christ on the cross does for us what his life and teachings cannot fully do. It brings us into a right relationship with God. This is why the cross is the central symbol of Christianity. God accepts the death of the Son of God as the means by which our sin is forgiven and our reconciliation with God is accomplished. Jesus freely offered himself as the sinless sacrifice to represent us, absorb our sin, bring us peace with God (Rom. 5:1), and "remove sin by the sacrifice of himself" (Heb. 9:26).

28. What is the meaning of the cross?

Presbyterians affirm that there is no one meaning to the cross of Christ. The cross is the focus of Christian faith because we believe it points to the inexhaustible riches of God's love. No words can capture all it means. No images or theories adequately convey its fullness and significance for the world and for each of us.

Yet theologians (of course!) have tried to say what the cross means. Theologically, the death of Jesus Christ on the cross is called the "atonement." This term means God and humanity are made "at-one" through the offering of Jesus, who died for us (1 Thess. 5:9–10).

The Christian church has never said there is only one "correct" view of the atonement. Some important ways of understanding the meaning of the cross are:

Christ Is Victor. In his death on the cross, Christ won victory over the powers that enslave humanity: sin, death, and Satan. Christ offers himself as the sinless sacrifice. It appeared that evil was victorious on the cross, but God raised Christ in the resurrection and thus defeated the evil "rulers and authorities" by "triumphing over them" (Col. 2:15).

Satisfaction for Sin. A key theory of the atonement in Western Christianity sees the cross as the place where Christ satisfied God's law and justice. Sinful humans stand guilty before God and cannot save themselves. Only one who is perfectly obedient to God's law and is sinless could offer himself as a substitute for sinners, to justify them in God's sight. Jesus, the sinless Son of God, died on the cross to fulfill the demands of God's law, justice, and even wrath against sin (Rom. 5:18–21). Now God sees sinners through the righteousness of Christ.

Example to Follow. An alternative view stresses not a change in how God views sinners as a result of Christ's death, but how the cross is the supreme example of God's suffering love and the power of God's goodness to triumph over sin. When we see the depths of God's love by looking at the cross, we are awakened, desire to forsake sin, and achieve reconciliation with God by determining to live with Christ as our example and showing similar love to others (1 John 4:11). Jesus is the most profound demonstration of God's vast love, and profoundly changes our lives.

The cross of Christ can mean different things to us at different points in our lives. We will never exhaust its richness. Regardless of what theological view one holds, we affirm with the hymn writer Isaac Watts that in the cross we find "Love so amazing, so divine, demands my soul, my life, my all."

29. Did Jesus really rise from the dead, and what does his resurrection mean?

Just as the cross of Christ is a mystery, in that we cannot fully capture or explain its meaning and power, so also is the resurrection of Jesus Christ from the dead. Presbyterians affirm this central doctrine of Christian faith, expressed simply in the Apostles' Creed, where we confess of Christ that he "rose again from the dead."

Some throughout history have found this hard to believe. After all, how many of our friends have come back from the dead recently? Yet this is precisely the point. Jesus Christ was divine and human. What is impossible for human power alone to accomplish can be carried out by the power of God. This is the Christian claim about the resurrection of Christ. God raised Jesus from the dead (Rom. 10:9; 1 Cor. 6:14, 15:4; Gal. 1:1). This is an event that happened in history, though it is totally unique from all other "historical events," as we refer to the normal "facts" of history today. As a result of the resurrection of Jesus: The Christian church emerged; the dejected disciples of Jesus were transformed into apostles of joy; and the Christian community met together for worship on the first day of the week in celebration of the resurrection—a major departure from their Jewish roots of Sabbath worship.

The death of a human person has no power to bring salvation. But the death of the eternal Son of God, who was vindicated in his life and death by his resurrection—this brings salvation! Jesus died on the cross but "was raised for our justification" (Rom. 4:25).

God raised Jesus from the dead. This means, among much else, that Jesus is alive forevermore and that we can have fellowship with him. The power of sin and death are forever defeated by Jesus' resurrection, and God's final victory at the end of history is secured. Evil will not prevail! The resurrection makes our full redemption possible. It gives meaning to Christ's death, assuring us that the cross truly has the power to transform our relationships with God and with others (Phil. 3:10). The resurrection enables us to have a union with the living Christ through faith and "if we have been united with him in a death like his, we will certainly be united with him in a resurrection like his" (Rom. 6:5). Christ's resurrection power enables us to "walk in newness of life" (Rom. 6:4) and gives us the "living hope" of our own resurrection (1 Pet. 1:3). For "we know that the one who raised the Lord Jesus will raise us also with Jesus" (2 Cor. 4:14), to live now and forever!

5

Humanity

30. What is the purpose of life?

One of life's biggest questions is the meaning of it all: What is the purpose of life? To make it personal: What is the purpose of my life? Thoughtful people consider this at some point. It's basic and sets our directions in countless ways.

Presbyterians have inherited a famous snapshot answer. The Westminster Shorter Catechism, from the seventeenth century, poses the question this way: "What is man's chief end?" The answer: "Man's chief end is to glorify God, and to enjoy him forever" (*BC* 7.001; a child got it wrong with the response: "to endure him forever"!).

The Catechism capsulizes the biblical view that humans are to live in relationship with God our creator, and that we are to love and serve the God we know in Jesus Christ, by the power of the Holy Spirit.

Paul captured this motivation when he instructed the Corinthians: "Whatever you do, do everything for the glory of God" (1 Cor. 10:31). This was the passion of the psalmist who wrote: "And there is nothing on earth that I desire other than you" (Ps. 73:25).

Single-hearted devotion to bringing glory to God is a comprehensive "game plan" for life. The God we know in Jesus Christ, as our Creator and Redeemer, is the one we serve with our whole heart, soul, mind, and strength (Mark 12:30; Deut. 6:5). We want to bring "every thought captive to obey Christ" (2 Cor. 10:5) so we can live as God's people, honoring God and carrying out God's

desires for this world. We want to obey God's will and devote ourselves to the praise and purposes to which God calls us. This is the
big picture for our life's aim. It is the agenda ultimately worth our
efforts. It is the only direction that makes life fully meaningful and
significant. This is the way God created us to live, with the priorities and purposes God wants us to have.

The result? We enjoy God—now and forever. Our deepest
delight is God's presence with us. What else ultimately matters?
God created us to enjoy our relationship with the one who gives
purpose and meaning, the one who loves us and "holds us by the
hand" (Ps. 37:24).

31. What does it mean to say humans are created in the image of God?

The biblical accounts of creation portray humans as created by
the power of God (Gen. 1–2). The Scripture also indicates that
humans are created "in the image of God" (Gen. 1:26–27). Most
basically, this defines who humans are. We are creatures of God
and created in and for a relationship with God.

There have been various ways of understanding what the phrase
"image of God" means. Some have said we should understand it
in terms of the characteristics that humans share with God. These
would include things like rationality, freedom, dominion, and so
on. Some have made a distinction between the "image" of God and
the "likeness" of God, since Gen. 1:26 says: "Let us make
humankind in our image, according to our likeness." In this view,
"image" relates to our intellect or reason and "likeness" to our
"righteousness," or relationship with God.

There is no one Presbyterian view on this matter. Most simply,
we can understand the idea that humans are created in the "image
of God" if we say that we are created to enjoy a relationship with
our creator. As humans, we are inextricably connected to God our
creator. We are not intended by our creator to live isolated lives.

Also, we can read "image of God" as a verb. As humans we are
"to image" God. We are to reflect and represent God our creator.

The most important fact of our human condition is that all persons are created to live in relationship with our creator and we are all created to point toward God, or "mirror" God, so that we "image" God. When people see us, they should see God reflected in us. This is God's intention in creating us. It is seen clearly in Jesus. Our sad story, as humans, is that the image of God in us has been spoiled by sin.

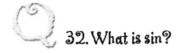

32. What is sin?

If we are created in the image of God, to represent and reflect God, then sin is our breaking of this image. Sin is the perversion and distortion of the image of God in us, so that we do not live in the type of relationship that God intended in creation. The first two chapters of the book of Genesis tell us of our creation by God. Chapter 3 is the story of sin's intrusion into the good creation.

Sin means what we are and what we do that is contrary to God. This is sin's essential character. Presbyterians believe that sin is both our nature now as humans, our "condition," as well as the actions we do (or fail to do) that are opposed to what God intends for us as humans. Whatever else is true of us, we are "not the people we should be."

There are a number of biblical expressions for sin. We rupture our personal relationship with God by the things we do that alienate us from our loving creator. Sin enslaves us as the human race and as individuals in its addictive power. Sin as our human condition and as what we do makes us unclean and unworthy to stand in the sight of our holy and righteous creator. Sin means the pursuing of our personal goals and agendas in life, seeking our own self-interests rather than God's or the good of our neighbor. Sin also makes us guilty people in God's sight, since we have not followed either God's will or God's law for how God intends us to live. Sin may also mean that we retreat within ourselves and fail to act at times, when honoring the image of God in other persons would mean we should act in their behalf. So we "miss the mark" and fail to be who God wants us to be. We may seek to live "my way" instead of "God's way," as people who image their creator. The Bible indicates "all have sinned and fall short of the glory of God" (Rom. 3:23). The consequences of sin are to be cut off from God, and ultimately death (Rom. 6:23).

33. Why do we sin?

There is no correct reason to explain why people sin. We've all had this experience: we know what is right, but we don't do it. For no apparent "reason," we turn away from the good and embrace the bad. We turn from what we know is God's will to do what we know is wrong or sinful in God's sight.

This is sometimes called the "riddle of sin." There are no good grounds or sensible motives for human sin. Sin is rebellion against God, breaking God's laws, asserting our own wills over God's will. Yet we know that sin is senseless. It does not ultimately help us—it further ruptures our relationship with God. Yet, sin we do. Even Paul confessed, "I do not do the good I want, but the evil I do not want is what I do" (Rom. 7:19).

This enigma of human sinning is seen in the story of Adam and Eve in the garden of Eden. There they enjoyed complete delight. They had an uninterrupted relationship with their creator. All their needs were met; they were in "paradise." The only stipulation was that they obey God's command not to eat from "the tree of the knowledge of good and evil" (Gen. 2:15–17). Yet this is what happened. Adam and Eve disobeyed God. They were tempted by the serpent, ate from the tree, and then faced the consequences: they were banished from the garden and lost its benefits, including their perfect relationship with God. Finally they met death for their actions—even as we do today as human beings.

We still sin. Theologically, Presbyterians believe we have inherited "original sin," so that we are all sinners by nature. But the prior question of why any human should want to sin is still an enigma. Sin is senseless. There is no meaning to be found to make sin "explicable." We see the stupidity of sin and its results when Jesus said of those who put him to death (and to all of us as sinners): "They hated me without a cause" (John 15:25; Ps. 69:4).

There is no self-excuse for sin. By seeking a reason or trying to explain our motives, we aim to deflect our blame or shift responsibility off our shoulders. In the face of this, there is one path. We can only confess our sin, admit our guilt, renounce our actions, and turn to God in repentance and trust. For God loves us and will "abundantly pardon" (Isa. 55:7).

34. Do Presbyterians believe that humans are totally evil?

No. We believe that humans are sinful and that sin affects all the dimensions of our lives. But humans are not totally evil in the sense of being so perverse, corrupt, and dangerous that there can be no order in society or no good purposes served.

Traditionally, Presbyterian theology has spoken of "total depravity." This is a way of saying that sin is pervasive throughout our lives and sin dominates every area of our lives. This means there are no arenas that are exempt from the influence that our sinful nature exercises. Sinful humans need salvation for our whole selves. If this were not so, and there were some areas not touched by sin, then presumably they would be dimensions of the self that would be excepted from the need of salvation. But in the Presbyterian understanding of Scripture, no such areas exist. "Depravity" or "sinfulness" extends throughout the whole person. Groups of persons—institutions, governments, cultures, and society—since they are composed of sinful humans, are also affected by the power of sin. Sin can become institutionalized, as with racism and sexism. Sin as idolatry, or worshiping something other than the true God, can be both a personal and a corporate expression of this totality of sinfulness.

At the same time, humans are capable of making decisions that can serve a larger group in a positive manner, even when these decisions are infected by self-interest and human pride, which are also expressions of sin. Societies and cultures can function. The arts and human achievements can be celebrated. Theologians refer to this as God's "common grace." It is God's grace extended to sinful humans, whereby the power of sin is restrained and good results from human efforts can be enjoyed. This "grace" does not bring salvation or a right relationship with God. But it does allow for a civic society and for "sinners" to make important contributions to the common good.

35. What do we mean by original sin?

Original sin is a term to say that we are sinful in our "origins," as the human race.

The story of the entrance of sin into the world is conveyed in Genesis 3. Adam and Eve are portrayed as living in the garden of delight, enjoying a perfect relationship with God their creator. When temptation comes and the choice is made to disobey God's command not to eat of the "tree of the knowledge of good and evil" (Gen. 2:17), bad consequences follow. For their disobedience, Adam and Eve are expelled from the garden, and the relationship of trust and obedience they had with God is broken.

The results of this sin are pervasive. The apostle Paul said that "just as sin came into the world through one man, and death came through sin, . . . so death spread to all because all have sinned" (Rom. 5:12), and that "all die in Adam" (1 Cor. 15:22). Theologians who have been influential in the Presbyterian tradition have interpreted this to mean that the results of sin, from our "first parents" (whoever they were) have spread to affect all who have come after in the human family. As Paul indicates, "One man's trespass led to condemnation for all" (Rom. 5:18). The psalmist pointed to this reality when he wrote, "I was born guilty, a sinner when my mother conceived me" (Ps. 51:5).

We do not believe, as did St. Augustine in the fourth century, that original sin is passed on from one generation to another by the physical act of procreation. But as humans we have received a sinful nature that affects who we are and what we do. Our sinful actions are done because of our sinful natures. As humans, we are born sinners. This sin affects the totality of our lives and existence, including our minds, wills, and affections. Our sinful nature cuts us off from God, since it defaces the image of God in which we were created. As sinners, we are corrupt in relation to God's law and God's righteousness. We seek our own wills rather than God's will for our lives. We deserve God's condemnation, and stand under the sentence of death.

36. Do we have "free will"?

The answer to this question depends on how we define "free will." We can speak of the choices we make in everyday life. If we use the term this way, to describe the things we choose to do like go to bed, or pick up a box, or drink milk—we can say we have freedom of choice. What we do is done on the basis of our power to make decisions. Our will cannot be coerced or forced to do something that it does not want to do. No power on earth can make that happen.

But theologians have used the term "free will" in another sense. This is the question: "Do we have the power to do the good?" Or can we, by our own "will," do what God wills for us or choose to live the way God wants us to live? Immediately we see that the stakes are much higher here. We are talking about things that are really important. We are talking about spiritual choices and whether we as humans can will to do the good that God intends.

To this question, Presbyterians, along with Lutherans and others, have said, "No." By ourselves we do not have the "freedom" to choose to follow God's ways. We do not have the "free will" to will the good or God's will in our lives.

Why? We do not have this freedom of the will because of our sin. The power of sin affects our minds, hearts, wills, and affections. This power is so strong that it prevents us from choosing God's ways. We are sinners by nature. Our actions—and our wills—are expressions of our natures. What we do reflects who we are. And we are persons infected by the virus of sin so strongly that the totality of our lives is under sin's power. Without God's help to give us new wills and hearts and minds, in Jesus Christ, we will always choose the sinful path. We will not be interested in God's love in Jesus Christ, since we are unable to act in any other than our sinful ways. Our wills are in bondage to sin. Our only hope is for God's gracious love to do for us what we cannot do for ourselves—give us the wills to have faith and trust in God.

6

Holy Spirit

Some years ago, a theologian wrote a book called *The Shy Member of the Trinity*. This was a book about the Holy Spirit. Presbyterians often speak about God and Jesus, but less often, it seems, about the Holy Spirit.

We believe vigorously in the Holy Spirit as a coequal member of the Trinity, sharing the divine essence with God the Father and God the Son. We believe the Holy Spirit is a person, one who can be known and who relates to us and affects us in our everyday lives. The Bible has much to say about the Spirit. But the reason for the book title is that the Spirit is portrayed in Scripture not as drawing self-attention, but supremely as a "witness" to Jesus Christ. The Spirit points to God's self-revelation in the person of Jesus and operates to make the knowledge of Jesus Christ known.

This is seen in two major aspects of the Spirit's activity: the Spirit's work in relation to Scripture and the Spirit's work in relation to salvation.

We confess that the Scriptures are "inspired" by God (2 Tim. 3:16) and that persons who were "moved by the Holy Spirit spoke from God" (2 Pet. 1:21). The church confesses the Spirit was operative in the writing of Scripture, in the shaping of the biblical texts, their transmission, and in helping us today, as believers to interpret the Bible. We should always pray before we read Scripture, asking the same Spirit who inspired the Bible to help us interpret God's Word today.

The Holy Spirit also plays a primary role in salvation. Presbyterians have particularly emphasized this aspect of the Spirit's work. We believe the Holy Spirit illuminates sinners, giving them the gift of faith in Jesus Christ. We come to confess Jesus Christ as Lord and Savior by the work of the Holy Spirit. The work of illumination that brings faith is followed in Christian experience by the ongoing indwelling of the Spirit in the church and in the lives of Christians, leading, guiding, comforting, challenging, and equipping God's people to serve Jesus Christ. We never know the ways in which the Spirit will move us into new modes of mission and ministry. "The Spirit is the one that testifies [witnesses], for the Spirit is the truth" (1 John 5:6).

38. In what ways does the Holy Spirit work in the church?

Presbyterians believe the Holy Spirit is active in the church as well as in our personal lives. Theologically, the Spirit works in sanctification, our growth in Christian faith and life (2 Thess. 2:13; 1 Cor. 6:11). As we mature in the faith, we perceive the Holy Spirit at work. When the church carries out its mission and ministries in the world, we see the Spirit's work to make the gospel of Jesus Christ known in word and deed. So the Holy Spirit is tremendously energetic! The Spirit brings us to faith in Christ for salvation, unites us with Christ, and calls the church together as the people of God. The ongoing work of the Spirit is to lead and guide Christian believers in the church while equipping us to serve as Christ's disciples in the world.

In short, the Holy Spirit sustains us in carrying out Christ's ministry. The Spirit equips the church with "gifts" to enable our ministries (1 Cor. 12:4–11). The Spirit leads us into ways of service to enact Christ's forgiving, reconciling, liberating, and compassionate word. The Spirit enables love to be shared (Gal. 5:22; Rom. 5:5). The Spirit makes the characteristics of God's kingdom present realities: righteousness, peace, and joy (Rom. 14:17; 8:6).

Presbyterians recognize the full range of the Holy Spirit's activities, both inside and outside the church. This makes the Christian life exciting! We never know what directions the Spirit will prompt us toward, or into what new ministries the Spirit will lead us. Our joy in being obedient to God (Acts 5:32) is strengthened by the assurance that we are the children of God (Rom. 8:14) and live in the "communion" of the Holy Spirit (2 Cor. 13:13). We participate in the Spirit's activities as the Spirit uses us to be the means of representing the reign of God in the world by the church's proclamation, fellowship, and service. The Spirit unifies the church in Jesus Christ (Eph. 4:5) and enables us to continue our ministries with joy, even in the midst of persecutions (1 Thess. 1:6). The Spirit helps us in prayer (Rom. 8:26–27), and the Spirit's presence with us helps us anticipate the glorious future that God has prepared (2 Cor. 1:22; Rom. 8:17).

So Presbyterians are people of the Spirit! We are sustained by the Spirit, rely on the Spirit, and are led by the Spirit. We have the hope that "does not disappoint us, because God's love has been poured into our hearts through the Holy Spirit that has been given to us" (Rom. 5:5).

39. What do we believe about the "baptism of the Holy Spirit"?

Some Christian traditions distinguish between "water baptism" and the "baptism of the Holy Spirit." In the New Testament, the Spirit is associated with baptism (Acts 2:38; 1 Cor. 6:11; 12:13; Titus 3:5–7). Yet questions about the relation of the Spirit to baptism remain. Some see these two "baptisms" as distinct and separate. Others have linked them together.

Contemporary churches in the Anabaptist and the Pentecostal traditions typically distinguish between an "inner baptism" of the Holy Spirit and an "outward baptism" by water. The inner baptism is the experience of salvation, to be followed by a public profession of faith marked by water baptism. Some Anabaptist groups in the past emphasized that the baptism of the Spirit will entail suffering. Pentecostalism typically sees the "baptism of the Spirit" as a joyful event, which also brings with it certain "spiritual gifts," including often glossolalia, or speaking in tongues.

Presbyterians have usually seen the sacrament of baptism as the sign and seal of the outpouring of God's Spirit into one's life. Faith and repentance are marks of the genuineness of the Spirit's work, of which the sacrament of baptism is the expression. The outward "sign" (water) and inward reality (the gift of God's Holy Spirit) are united in the sacrament. Presbyterians do not look for a separate "experience" of the Holy Spirit (a "baptism") apart from the sacrament of baptism administered in the church. Children baptized as infants are received into the covenant community of the church, and in baptism the parents acknowledge faith and pledge to raise the child with a knowledge of the gospel. The Spirit is given to children in baptism in anticipation of the faith and repentance they will express later as they confirm the vows the parents made for them (confirmation). Children of believers belong to Christ through election. Baptism and faith confirm this reality, given in Jesus Christ.

So, the "baptism of the Holy Spirit" is best understood as testifying to the reality of what Presbyterians believe occurs in baptism. Baptism signifies our new birth by the power of the Holy Spirit who is given to us, our new life in Jesus Christ through faith, and our commitment to share in the church's life and ministry as Christ's disciples.

40. What do Presbyterians believe about the "gifts of the Holy Spirit"?

Presbyterians believe we become Christians by the work of the Holy Spirit, who is with us in the church and in our Christian experience as we live as disciples of Jesus Christ (Acts 2:38). The Spirit equips the church and its members for ministry and gives "spiritual gifts" so the ministries of Jesus Christ can be carried out in and through the church (1 Cor. 2:12; 12:1; Heb. 2:4).

These spiritual gifts are marked by wide variety (Rom. 12:3–8). Yet all come from the same Spirit (1 Cor. 12:4–11). There are diversities of activities in which church members engage as they carry out their ministries—led, strengthened, and nourished by the Spirit.

The point of using the gifts of the Holy Spirit is to serve "the common good" in the church (1 Cor. 12:7). This spectrum of gifts enables the church to carry out a panorama of ministries as the spiritual gifts of its members are engaged and enacted. Paul urges Christians to "strive for the greater gifts" (12:31), to "pursue love and strive for the spiritual gifts" (14:1), and to "strive to excel in them" for the purpose of "building up the church" (14:12). It is clear that gifts given by the Holy Spirit are not intended to bring praise or glory to the recipient, but rather to be put to use so Jesus Christ is glorified and served through the church. This perspective enables gifts to be received in gratitude and also to be recognized as means to a greater end, the service of Christ. This is the ultimate purpose of the Spirit's gifts, that "some would be apostles, some prophets, some evangelists, some pastors and teachers, to equip the saints for the work of ministry, for building up the body of Christ" (Eph. 4:11–12).

All Christians receive the Holy Spirit as we receive Jesus Christ and are blessed by the grace of God's Spirit's gifts to us. They are not restricted to only one particular or "special" spiritual gift. We have "callings" or activities through which we can use our many gifts, as well as personalities through which our gifts may be expressed as the "fruit of the Spirit" (Gal. 5:22–25). Our gifts are "activated by one and the same Spirit, who allots to each one individually just as the Spirit chooses" (1 Cor. 12:11). Presbyterians believe we receive spiritual gifts from the Holy Spirit with gratitude and joy!

41. Is "speaking in tongues" a necessary sign of the Holy Spirit in one's life?

Some Christian traditions, particularly the Pentecostal, stress the gift of "speaking in tongues" (also called "glossolalia," from the Greek word *glōssa* meaning "tongue"). This refers to a person's uttering words in a language unknown to the speaker, and is seen as a gift of the Holy Spirit. If this happens in the context of a worship service, there may also be someone who is given the gift of "interpretation," to be able to say what is being said. This was a practice that occurred in the early church, even on the day of Pentecost, when people spoke in unknown languages and were also able to understand such languages (Acts 2:4–13).

The apostle Paul refers to this phenomenon (1 Cor. 14:2). But he recognizes it is not a gift for every Christian (1 Cor. 12:30) and that it is useful only when someone can interpret what is said so the church can be upbuilt. In this regard, the gift of "prophecy," in which the word and will of God can be proclaimed, is more useful and greater (1 Cor. 14:5). Paul refers to his own experience (1 Cor. 14:18), but also recognizes that those outside the church who might view this experience will have no idea what is going on! (1 Cor. 14:23).

Presbyterians have not stressed the gift of "speaking in tongues." Some have even doubted that it is a legitimate activity now, believing that these kinds of "exceptional gifts" of the Holy Spirit are no longer given to today's church. However, some Presbyterians have experienced this gift. Yet, all Presbyterians should acknowledge that this is not a gift that is "required" as an indubitable sign of the Holy Spirit in one's life.

There is a bigger New Testament picture of the work of the Holy Spirit in the church and Christian experience. Paul sees the gifts of the Spirit as expressing themselves in the "fruit of the Spirit," which is the visible manifestation of the Spirit's presence. The "fruit of the Spirit" is very "ordinary" phenomena: "love, joy, peace, patience, kindness, generosity, faithfulness, gentleness, and self-control" (Gal. 5:22–23). These are the signs of the Spirit's presence. The greatest gift of God's Spirit is love, which is the crucial ingredient, even if one speaks in "the tongues of mortals and of angels" (1 Cor. 13:1, 13).

42. What is the Holy Spirit's role in evangelism?

Presbyterians strongly affirm the primary role of the Holy Spirit in evangelism. Typically we define evangelism as the sharing of the "evangel," or the gospel, of Jesus Christ. The "good news" of the reign of God that Jesus proclaimed during his ministry (Matt. 9:35; 10:7) is the "good news of Jesus Christ" himself (Mark 1:1), in his life, death, and resurrection (2 Cor. 10:14). This gospel was proclaimed by the early apostles (Acts 8:25; 14:7) and is the message of God's grace in Jesus Christ (Acts 20:24) to be shared with the whole world (Matt. 28:18–20).

We believe we come to believe this message of the gospel through the illuminating work of the Holy Spirit. The Spirit gives us the gift of faith that transforms our lives. The Spirit opens our hearts and minds, turning them from the enslaving power of sin to embrace the promise of God's loving grace and mercy in Jesus Christ. The Spirit makes us a "new creation" (2 Cor. 5:17), regenerates or renews us (Titus 3:5), and sanctifies us, so we can grow in faith (2 Thess. 2:13). "Through the Spirit, by faith, we eagerly wait for the hope of righteousness" (Gal. 5:5).

Presbyterian theology has always recognized that what happens when we share the gospel of Jesus Christ in evangelism does so by the work of the Holy Spirit. When people believe in Jesus Christ, repent of their sins, experience conversion, and begin to walk in a new direction in a life of love and service to Jesus Christ—they do so because the Holy Spirit has been at work. We trust the Spirit to bring forth faith and new life. It is the Spirit who "converts" people—never a preacher! The Holy Spirit brings the truth of the gospel "home" to us and enables us to receive the message of the gospel of Jesus Christ by faith.

It is important to recognize this primacy of the Spirit in evangelism. This perspective enables us to realize that the results of our efforts to spread the gospel rest with the Spirit. The church proclaims the gospel as vigorously and faithfully as we can. But it is ultimately the Holy Spirit who enables our witness to Jesus Christ to bring faith and new life. This comforts us, but also challenges us to be energetic, innovative, and joyful. For we realize that God can and does use our efforts to bring the transforming gospel of Jesus Christ into the lives of others.

43. Does the Holy Spirit work outside the church?

The Holy Spirit is God present with us. The Spirit gives gifts to the church (1 Cor. 12:7–13). The Spirit is received by faith (Gal. 3:14). Believers are "baptized with the Holy Spirit" to become leaders in the church (Acts 11:16).

But the Spirit of God is also active in creation at large and in ways that go beyond what the Spirit does in and through the church. We can see the Spirit's working wherever the Spirit's goals and purposes are being carried out.

For example, when Jesus attended the synagogue in his home-town of Nazareth, he read from the prophet Isaiah (61:1–2) and said:

> "The Spirit of the Lord is upon me,
>   because he has anointed me
>   to bring good news to the poor.
> He has sent me to proclaim release to the captives
>   and recovery of sight to the blind,
>   to let the oppressed go free,
> to proclaim the year of the Lord's favor."
>
> (Luke 4:18–19)

Here Jesus' ministry was being previewed. We find in his words what types of actions the Holy Spirit of God desires to carry out.

If so, one way of understanding the wider work of the Holy Spirit in the world is to see the ways and places where the poor receive "good news," where those who are captive to powers (we could say such as to addictions) are released, where those who are blind (in whatever sense) recover their sight, and where the oppressed go free. Where the Lord's favor is proclaimed, there the Spirit of God is at work.

To see the Spirit's work in this way enables Presbyterians to be alert to God's wider work in the world, and encourages us to join with all peoples in struggles for peace, justice, and freedom. We will sense an awareness of God in the Spirit as we cooperate, even with those who are not Christians, in the work and purposes of God in society and culture. We will watch for the surprising work of God's Spirit, even in times and places and among people we do not expect.

7

Salvation

44. What is the grace of God?

The grace of God means the "unmerited favor" God extends to us as sinners. It is sometimes defined in two ways: Grace is God's giving us what we don't deserve; and grace is God's not giving us what we do deserve.

The psalmist declared: "But you, O Lord, are a God merciful and gracious, slow to anger and abounding in steadfast love and faithfulness" (Ps. 86:15; see also 103:8). God's "grace," as gracious Lord, is associated with other characteristics of God. The pleas for God to be gracious (Ps. 4:1; 25:16; 41:10) are uttered because this is who God is: a God who extends grace. For God "does not deal with us according to our sins, nor repay us according to our iniquities" (Ps. 103:10). God does not give us what we do deserve because of our sin—ultimately, separation from God and death (Rom. 6:23). God gives us what we do not deserve—forgiveness and mercy (Dan. 9:9).

The grace of God is found most clearly in Jesus Christ. He is God's grace "in person." Through his life, death, and resurrection, God's grace has been extended to humanity to bring salvation. Through Christ, we have a restored relationship with God, our sin is forgiven, and as followers of Christ we live daily by God's continuing grace. We are called by God's grace (2 Tim. 1:9), "saved" by God's grace (Eph. 2:5–9), "justified" by grace (Rom. 3:24; Titus 3:7), and given gifts by God's grace (Rom. 12:6) to be used in the church for the common good (1 Cor. 12:4–11). In other words, our whole salvation depends on God's grace! This is why one of Martin Luther's slogans during the Protestant Reformation was *sola gratia*—"by grace alone."

Theologically, we call God's act in Christ God's "special" grace. God has provided salvation to undeserving sinners and does not execute the divine judgment we rightly deserve.

Some in our Presbyterian tradition have also spoken of God's "common grace," which is God's restraint of sin—so societies and cultures can exist and not be totally destroyed by human sin. God's common grace enables us to celebrate the arts and sciences and enjoy life—another form of God's graciousness in reaching out to us as God's creation.

45. What does it mean to be "saved"?

To be "saved" is to experience Christian salvation. The Bible clearly indicates that God has been at work to undo the damage done by sin in the human family (Gen. 3). Sin has fractured and disrupted the love, trust, and obedience God intended for humans to experience in our relationship with our creator and our fellow humans. Our lives are marked by seeking our own agendas, glory, and power, instead of God's.

God has been at work to overcome the destructive powers of sin. God called the people of Israel into existence and into a covenant relationship to be God's people, and promised Abraham that through his offspring "all the nations of the earth gain blessing for themselves" (Gen. 22:18). God established other covenants with persons such as David, drawing Israel into a place of privilege and responsibility. God promised a Messiah. Jeremiah the prophet anticipated a "new covenant" in coming days, when God will "forgive their iniquity, and remember their sin no more" (Jer. 31:31–34).

We Presbyterian Christians believe sin is forgiven and a restored relationship with God is established through the person and work of Jesus Christ. He is the Messiah. Through his life, death, and resurrection, we have been given the gift of salvation. Salvation is expressed in the New Testament through a number of different images, such as peace with God, reconciliation, redemption, justification, and other terms. All point to a new relationship with God as being established through Jesus Christ. Sin and its power are overcome. God and humanity are brought together as God originally intended. Through faith in Jesus Christ we experience the presence of God, a union with Christ, and the power of the Holy Spirit in our lives. Those who are saved are called together in the Christian church, where God is worshiped and served. The love, trust, and obedience God desires is now made possible. We have "eternal life" through God's gift in Jesus Christ. This is the "gospel," the good news of our salvation (Eph. 1:13). Our lives are transformed, we live to serve Christ, and we carry out God's will in mission and ministry to the world. All this, plus the hope laid for us in heaven that comes to us in the gospel of salvation (Col. 1:5).

46. Must we be baptized in order to be saved?

Christian baptism is ordinarily a part of Christian salvation. Baptism is a sign of salvation, of the incorporation of believers into Jesus Christ through faith. This union with Christ by faith is testified to by our baptism, which points to the spiritual reality of our being identified with Jesus Christ (Rom. 6:1–4). The rite of baptism is the important outward expression of this inward reality.

There are two extremes to avoid in answering whether or not we must be baptized in order to be saved. One is thinking that by participating in a ceremony of baptism, we are automatically guaranteed to be saved (or to experience "regeneration"). This is the view of Roman Catholics, Orthodox, and some Lutherans and Anglicans. The emphasis is on the rite administered by the church rather than on the characteristic of faith in those who are baptized.

The other extreme is the view that baptism is a dispensable act that has no role to play in salvation. Here, one does not need to be committed to the church or its sacraments. Salvation is seen as a wholly private activity. The life of faith may be lived apart from the community of faith in the church.

A Presbyterian perspective stresses the need for baptism as a key part of salvation and the life of faith, but stresses the need for personal faith as the crucial ingredient for the sacrament of baptism to have effect. Participating in the sacrament alone is no guarantee of salvation. We are saved solely by our personal faith in Jesus Christ (Rom. 1:16; 1 Pet. 1:9). Yet true faith in Christ propels us into the church to seek baptism as an outward expression of this genuine faith. Baptism is a sign for the world to see, indicating we belong to Christ, are identified with him, and are committed to live as Christ's followers and disciples. It is God's sign to us of God's electing love, which has brought us to faith. In baptism we acknowledge our election and commit ourselves to repentance and living lives of faith and obedience. So baptism is a vital part of our salvation experience. It is the crucial expression of our response to God's loving grace. It sets us on a life of discipleship as we are "baptized into one body" in the "one Spirit" (1 Cor. 12:13) as we move toward the "unity of the faith" (Eph. 4:13).

47. Will non-Christians be saved?

Presbyterians should always maintain that who is saved is decided solely by God. This is basic theology: God is free. God is free to give salvation to whomever God chooses. We believe this about election and predestination. We are saved only and solely by God's gracious choosing. We acknowledge that salvation belongs to God. Jesus commands us not to "judge" on these matters (Matt. 7:1). So, we ourselves do not know who will be saved.

At the same time, there are other theological perspectives to keep in mind.

First, salvation comes through faith in Jesus Christ (2 Tim. 3:15; 2:10; 1 Thess. 5:9). This is the basic message of the gospel. Jesus said, "I am the way, and the truth, and the life. No one comes to the Father except through me" (John 14:6). So, as Presbyterian Christians, we proclaim vigorously and persuasively that we come to salvation through Jesus Christ, God's Son, who was sent to save the world (John 3:16) and bring the benefits of salvation to all (Luke 3:6; Titus 2:11). Proclaiming this evangelical message is always imperative for us.

At the same time, we recognize God is free to give salvation in whatever way God chooses. Ultimately, we do not know for certain how God chooses to administer salvation in relation to those who have never heard the Christian gospel, those who have rejected the Christian gospel, or those of other religious faiths that do not perceive Jesus the same as we Christians do. God's freedom in relation to salvation is basic and necessary. We cannot prescribe to God that God either must or must not save any persons.

A third point to remember is that the Holy Spirit works more widely than we know. The wind of God's Spirit, said Jesus, "blows where it chooses" (John 3:8). We do not and cannot know those with whom and in whom the Spirit of God is at work.

The result of these perspectives is that Presbyterian Christians preach the gospel of Jesus Christ for salvation as energetically as possible, calling all people to faith in Jesus Christ. We do so while acknowledging God is free and is at work in ways we cannot know. We also remember the major intention of God, who "desires everyone to be saved and to come to the knowledge of the truth" (1 Tim. 2:4).

48. What is predestination?

Predestination and election are often used as synonymous terms to describe God's gracious initiation of the gift of salvation in Jesus Christ.

The New Testament fully affirms that God "predestines" persons to salvation (Rom. 8:29–30) and that the "elect" of God receive salvation (Mark 13:27; Rom. 8:33; 2 Tim. 2:10). God "chose us in Christ before the foundation of the world to be holy and blameless before him in love" (Eph. 1:4; Col. 3:12).

Presbyterians have emphasized election and predestination as a way of affirming that our salvation is totally due to the grace of God. We do not deserve to be saved; we cannot earn salvation. We are chosen by God to be God's people, and this is God's free act. We receive our election as a gift, graciously bestowed by God on us.

We need this electing action of God because of our sin. Presbyterians know the reality of the biblical picture of humans, who are "dead through . . . trespasses and sins" (Eph. 2:1, 5) and are unable to turn to God or respond to God's word by ourselves. We are sinners by nature, enslaved to sin's power, which affects every dimension of our lives. Our wills are captive to sin's control, making us effectively cut off from God and from all that is good.

Sin is so pervasive that it is impossible for us, on our own, to repent of our sin or seek the relationship of love and trust that God desires. In such a "hopeless" situation, we experience God's grace—God's reaching out to do for us what we cannot do for ourselves: saving us.

God saves us by grace, or we can say God chooses us, predestines us, elects us—by grace. This is the source of praise. Our salvation is due totally to the action of God in transforming our lives by the power of the Holy Spirit, giving us the gift of faith in Jesus Christ, and electing us by God's free mercy. Faith is not a human achievement, it is the "gift of God—not the result of works, so that no one may boast" (Eph. 2:8–9). We receive God's gift of election with deepest gratitude and joy. Right now we experience that of which the saints of God sing: "Salvation belongs to our God who is seated on the throne, and to the Lamb!" (Rev. 7:10).

49. Should I worry that I am not one of God's elect?

No. If you are worried enough to ask this question, chances are you shouldn't worry about being one of God's elect!

Why? Simply because in our traditional Presbyterian under-standing of election and predestination, we recognize that God saves sinners who do not in themselves even *want* to be saved. That is, we believe the powers of sin are so strong that they turn us away from God. Our whole lives and all their parts—hearts, minds, desires, wills—all are turned inward on ourselves instead of outward toward God. We are sinners by nature, addicted to sin, and our actions are expressions of our sinful wills.

If we are at the point of worrying about God in our lives and whether we are part of God's elect, it would seem to indicate God's Spirit is at work within us. If the Spirit were not active, we would not care about this question. We would continue in our sin, uncon-cerned about our relationship with God. Since we have this con-cern, we can surmise that God's Spirit is stirring within us, leading us to consider what otherwise would not be an issue at all.

A way to meet this worry or concern is to ask oneself this sim-ple question: "Do I believe in Jesus Christ?" If the answer to this is "No," then one will not long worry about whether one is of the elect. The concern will simply not be there.

If we can answer, "Yes, I believe in Jesus Christ as my Lord and Savior," then this is the confession that makes one a Christian, and thus one called and elected by God to salvation. Instead of worry-ing, speculatively, about one's election, our question can be focused directly on Jesus, who is the "mirror of our election" (John Calvin) and in whom the electing purposes of God are fulfilled.

If a person has already confessed Christ as Lord and Savior, that person's election is secure. It is the duty of all of us as Christians to "rekindle the gift of God" that is within us (2 Tim. 1:6), to con-firm our call and election (2 Pet. 1:10), and to look to Jesus who is "the pioneer and perfecter of our faith" (Heb. 12:2).

50. Can I lose my salvation?

Presbyterians believe in the "perseverance of the saints." This is a theological understanding of salvation to indicate that once we are saved, God continues to hold us in faith so our salvation will not be lost. Sometimes this is called "eternal security," meaning that our lives of faith in Jesus Christ are held secure by God's power throughout our lives, into eternity.

We believe this on the basis of God's faithfulness. God is trustworthy, and the promises God makes, God keeps. The apostle Paul said, "I am confident of this, that the one who began a good work among you will bring it to completion by the day of Jesus Christ" (Phil. 1:6). God, who gives us the gift of salvation as an act of free grace, will continue to hold us in that salvation until the "day of Jesus Christ"—forever. Jesus indicated the same when he said, "I give them eternal life, and they will never perish. No one will snatch them out of my hand" (John 10:28; cf. 10:29). If we are held in God's hands, we will not slip through God's fingers!

In the Methodist and various Baptist traditions, there is belief in "backsliding." This is the view that a Christian can lose salvation. Due to sin, the salvation once received may be lost. Our Presbyterian theology, however, affirms that because of God's unchangeable love and covenant faithfulness in Jesus Christ, God gives the gift of perseverance. We are held in salvation by God's power, not our own. God's Spirit seals us for the "day of redemption" (Eph. 4:30). There may be times and experiences in our lives where we sin, and sin grievously. There may be long periods where it appears that we have drifted away or "lost" our salvation in Christ. If someone who previously confessed faith in Christ comes to denounce Christ, it is a sign that the profession of faith was not genuine in the first place. But we do not "backslide" to the point of losing our salvation. When our confession of Christ is genuine and we are united to Christ through faith, God's Holy Spirit abides in us so that we never totally or finally fall away from God's grace. "Perseverance" does not give us a license to live however we please, without regard for God. Instead, it is a source of praise to the God who has graciously called us into salvation, who will continue to hold us in Christ throughout our whole lives and bring us finally to glorification in heaven.

8

Church

51. What does it mean to be a church "member"?

To be a church member is to express one's faith in Jesus Christ and the desire to be his disciple, to share his love, and to serve him as a part of the church as the body of Christ.

A most basic question to ask of anyone wishing to become a member of a Presbyterian church is: "Who is your Lord and Savior?" The reply is: "Jesus Christ is my Lord and Savior." Question: "Do you promise to be Christ's faithful disciple, obeying his Word and showing his love?" Answer: "I do."

In these questions and answers, a profound life-changing event is recognized. To become a member of a Presbyterian church is to proclaim publicly one's allegiance to Jesus Christ. It is to vow to live a life of discipleship in which one grows in faith and service to Christ, and, through the church, to the world. The church member assumes responsibility for supporting the church in a variety of ways: through worship, education, mission and ministry, stewardship of resources, financial contributions, and other means. The church is the place where one's Christian life "takes shape." Joined in fellowship with other believers in the body of Christ, the member of Christ's church is part of the "communion of saints"—of all Christian believers throughout the world—as well as part of a local congregation where one's faith in Christ is lived out daily.

While "joining" the church occurs through simple affirmations, it takes a lifetime to live out the implications of church membership. Uniquely, the church is the only organization where to become a member one has to admit one is unworthy of membership! To acknowledge Jesus Christ as our Lord and Savior is to confess our faith and trust in him—and not ourselves—for eternal salvation. It is to announce that one's life does not belong to oneself, but to our Lord Jesus Christ. This profession is made publicly as a witness to the world and as a visible confession of faith. One's commitment to the church is the implication of one's confession of faith in Christ. We do not live out our Christian discipleship alone, but in the community of believers who have also professed their faith in Jesus Christ as Lord and Savior.

52. Why is the church so full of "sinners"?

The church is full of sinners because the church is *for* sinners.

The New Testament picture of the church does not "touch up the negatives" when it comes to portraying what the earliest Christian churches were like. When we read the letters of the apostle Paul to the "saints" (Eph. 1:1; Col. 1:2) in all the various churches, we find that he is always addressing difficulties that have emerged. Sometimes these relate to the practices of the churches, sometimes to their beliefs, and sometimes to the personalities of people who were having squabbles or acting in unchristian ways (Phil. 4:2). Paul's theological insights had to be brought to bear on the very real problems of churches, not the least of which was that church members were not believing or behaving as he believed Christians should. They were sinners.

This is not surprising if, as Presbyterians, we recognize that Christians are "forgiven sinners." We are saved by God's grace in Jesus Christ, not by our human "works" (Eph. 2:8–9). But our salvation does not bring us perfection. We will not live a perfect Christian life. We will sin, even as Christians. Paul himself struggled with this in his own life. Hear his agony when he confessed to the church at Rome: "For I do not do the good I want, but the evil I do not want is what I do" (Rom. 7:19). Christians are saved by God's grace in Christ, but we are still sinners. Yet now, as Christians, we seek and find forgiveness through Christ.

The Christian church is the community of sinners who are saved by grace, and yet who stand in continuing need of God's gracious forgiveness in Christ and of the loving forgiveness of others against whom we sin. Church quarrels, schisms, hypocrisy, and failures to be Christlike are marks of churches, as anyone who is a church member can testify. Yet it is precisely here where God's grace can still abound. It is in the community of faith that sins can be confessed and forgiveness and reconciliation offered. There is a realism to our view of the church. We are church members, sinful though we be. But we are sinners who are saved by grace.

53. What are the "visible" and the "invisible" church?

The terms "visible" and "invisible" church have been used by theologians to make a distinction between the church that "everybody sees" and the church that is known "only to God."

When we join a Presbyterian (or any Christian) church, we unite ourselves with a fellowship of believers who are disciples of Jesus Christ. We take on certain responsibilities to live as disciples of Christ and to serve God and be part of a local congregation. This is the "visible church." It is the community of Christians who outwardly profess their faith in Christ and join together for worship, fellowship, education, and service.

Yet not all those who at some point confess their faith in Christ as Lord and Savior continue to be part of the church. They may attend worship for a while and then stop participating. They may not support the church in any way and eventually, over time, be removed from the church membership rolls. Outwardly, it appears that their professed faith in Christ was not genuine, in that it did not endure in such a way as to lead them into lives of active Christian discipleship.

The recognition that sometimes a confession of faith in Christ does not continue to make an impact in a person's life led the fourth-century theologian Augustine to speak of the "invisible" church. This is the group of believers in the church whose faith is genuine and who will not fall away from Christian faith. Augustine, and later John Calvin, referred to these as God's elect.

We can know who is part of the visible church—the names are on the membership rolls. But we cannot know who is part of the invisible church, since that group is known only to God. The invisible church, as the elect of God, extends through all the ages, so that now those who have died have entered into the "church triumphant" in heaven and continue to be, from our point of view, a part of the invisible church. We do not "see" them, but their lives were genuinely Christian lives and now they participate in the eternal praise of God that we will one day join.

54. What is the "priesthood of all believers"?

The "priesthood of all believers" is a phrase associated with Martin Luther in the sixteenth century, and is often related to his concern that all Christians can act in "priestly" ways—by praying to God directly, and not having to go through a church's "priest"—and that all believers may teach the Christian faith to others on the basis of their own reading of the Scriptures. Linked with Luther's view that we are justified by faith alone ("justification by faith"), the priesthood of all believers became a liberating feature of the Protestant Reformation, since it meant that individual believers had great freedom and were not forced to go to God through the church's priests, and could read and interpret the Bible for themselves.

Presbyterian theology recognizes the truth of Luther's perspectives. We go on, however, to see also that the church itself as the covenant community of God is a "chosen race, a royal priesthood" (1 Pet. 2:9; Rev. 1:6; 5:10). We are made "priests" through Jesus Christ, who is the only true priest (Heb. 3:1) and who has called us into our ministries through the new covenant he has established (1 Cor. 11:25).

This means that the church has a calling, or vocation, to be "priests" in that we have a corporate responsibility and a privilege as God's believing, covenant people. Our "priesthood" is to offer Jesus Christ to the world, offer ourselves as "a living sacrifice" (Rom. 12:1), and pray to God on behalf of our sisters and brothers in Christ as well as on behalf of the whole world (James 5:16). Individual congregations act as a microcosm of the whole church and carry out the mission and ministries of the church on behalf of God and God's kingdom in the person of Jesus Christ. To participate in the church is to have a "priestly" ministry to others and for others. Those ordained by the church as "ministers of the Word" carry out certain ministerial functions. But all members of the covenant community in the church as the people of God have our ministries to carry out as well. We all share in the corporate "priesthood of all believers."

55. Why do Presbyterian churches put such a stress on Christian education?

When Jesus was asked "which commandment in the law is the greatest?" he replied, "You shall love the Lord your God with all your heart, and with all your soul, and with all your mind" (Matt. 22:37; Mark 12:30; Luke: 10:27). In this Jesus was indicating that we are to bring to our faith in God the best thought and understanding of which we are capable, and we are to use all our intellectual capabilities to serve in our love for God.

Our Presbyterian tradition has taken this perspective seriously, and has historically stressed education generally, theological education for clergy and Christian education in the church for laity, very strongly. John Calvin began the Genevan Academy, which educated citizens and clergy. Churches in our tradition have been active in establishing colleges and universities. Local Presbyterian churches in the United States have long-established Sunday school programs as well as other innovative educational opportunities for children, youth, and adults. We emphasize education because we believe that, as the twentieth-century theologian Karl Barth put it,

"The knowledge of God is the service of God." As we learn of God, we are also serving God.

Another way to see this is in terms of a theological motto that is part of our Presbyterian tradition. It is inherited from Augustine, during the period of the early church. We believe that "faith leads to understanding." Our faith in Jesus Christ inevitably propels us into wanting to learn more of Christ, of God's actions, and of what is revealed in Holy Scripture. So we stress Bible study, theological study, and the whole panorama of topics that will help us better understand God, the world, humanity, and all that God does. We believe children of Christian parents should embark on a lifetime of learning, particularly learning about the fullness of the Christian faith. Adult Presbyterians also have strong responsibilities to grow in their faith by seeking further understanding. Without the stimulus of new ideas and perceptions, our Christian faith can stagnate and not be all it can be. Christian education in the church enhances our faith and leads us ever farther into obeying Jesus' prescription to love God "with all our minds."

56. What is the "mission" of the church?

Presbyterians have defined the "mission of the church" in many ways. In times past, there have been strong emphases on evangelism—the church is to proclaim the gospel of Jesus Christ. There have been emphases on planting churches—on extending the Christian church into the whole world. There have been emphases on building up the body of Christ—education and service by the church's members.

All these understandings have their place. A bigger umbrella under which to see the mission of the church is to consider that the church is a community that is sent into the world by Jesus Christ to represent the reign, or the kingdom, of God.

The church does this in many ways. The church represents the reign of God within its own community. It should be a fellowship that models the love and forgiveness Jesus embodied. It should "maintain the unity of the Spirit in the bond of peace" (Eph. 4:3). The church is the fellowship where we find a foretaste of God's coming kingdom.

The church represents the reign of God through its service. The church responds to human need both globally and locally, no matter what the need may be. In this too it follows its master, Jesus, who "went about doing good and healing all who were oppressed" (Acts 10:38). The church is the congregation of care for those in need, corporately and personally.

The church also represents the reign of God through its proclamation. Preaching and teaching the gospel of Jesus Christ is the church's response of gratitude for being the people of God, who receive God's reign among us as a gift. We witness to God's loving action in Jesus Christ and, like the healed man, we "cannot keep from speaking about what we have seen and heard" (Acts 4:20), for God has entrusted the "message of reconciliation to us" (2 Cor. 5:19).

A wise theologian said, "The church exists by mission as a fire exists by burning." The church is called and sent by God not only to "do" mission, but to "be" God's mission in the world, proclaiming, serving, and being the community God wants us to be.

57. What should be the church's relation to culture?

Christian churches have always struggled to understand how we should be related to the cultures in which we find ourselves. Through the centuries, churches have had to adapt to their circumstances in a variety of ways. When we look back at various times and situations, we may now judge that some of these adaptations have been good and faithful to the gospel. Others have not have been good decisions or right practices. Churches cannot escape adopting attitudes and actions in relation to their cultures. Even by avoiding the question, they are already taking a stance. So the issue is one to be understood and addressed.

Reformed and Presbyterian churches have sometimes been

categorized as among those Christian churches that bring to their contexts the vision of Jesus Christ as the transformer of culture. That is, when Presbyterians have been involved in their societies, taken leadership positions within it, and by their participation in society's institutions and structures have tried to influence these, they have done so out of the conviction that Jesus Christ can "mak[e] all things new" (Rev. 21:5). Ultimately, it is not until the reign of God fully comes that the transformative work of Jesus Christ will be fully accomplished. But, in the meantime, Presbyterians who have been involved in culture have believed we are called to be God's servants. We are called to bring Jesus Christ and his will to bear on all dimensions of human life and need. So Presbyterians have been leaders in education, health care, government, and other social causes. We believe God is at work through Christ and through the efforts of God's people to carry out the divine will for human societies, as well as for the church and for individuals.

Sometimes Reformed Christians have had to work in hostile cultures, such as in Germany prior to World War II, when Reformed churches made a powerful witness to Jesus Christ through the Barmen Declaration (*BC* 8.0). Other times, we have failed miserably and been unfaithful to the gospel by capitulating to cultural idolatries and opposing what we can now see to be God's will. So the church must always be in prayer, seeking God's guidance, while proclaiming Jesus Christ and enacting the gospel of him "who fills all in all" (Eph. 1:23).

9

Worship

58. Why should we worship?

Worship is a human response to the divine. It is giving "worth," "praise," or "honor" to what is greater than we are. When we invest a being or object with value or allegiance, we "worship" in some degree. When we devote our lives to a person or institution or practice, we are investing that "object" of worship with what we value most—ourselves.

These aspects of "worship" have special significance in Christian faith, where worship is to be offered to God alone. Presbyterians take worship very seriously because we recognize that worship is the most important thing we do. Here the Holy Spirit calls people together to respond to the God revealed in the Old and New Testaments and supremely in Jesus Christ. We ascribe worth, praise, and honor to God, proclaiming God's greatness for who God is. We worship for what God has done, in the history of Israel and in sending Jesus Christ for our salvation. We proclaim our allegiance to God, the One of highest value in our lives. We worship out of profound gratitude, in awe, reverence, and devotion. We celebrate who God is and what God does. We "make a joyful noise to the LORD . . . worship the LORD with gladness," and "come into his presence with singing," for we "know that the LORD is God. It is he that made us, and we are his; we are his people, and the sheep of his pasture" (Ps. 100:1–3).

Presbyterians seek to worship God "in spirit and truth" (John 4:24). We believe God desires that "all things should be done decently and in order" (1 Cor. 14:40), including worship. So Presbyterians stress that there should be a theologically grounded order for worship. In worship we rehearse salvation history. In worship, the community of faith assembles in God's name, God's word is proclaimed, the people give thanks to God and go out into the world in God's name. Worship is marked by praise, proclamation, remembrance, and prayer. It is our most essential human activity. It is not an option, but an absolute necessity. Worship is the service of God's glory. We commit our lives to furthering the ministry of Jesus Christ, to living for God's glory, and following as the Holy Spirit guides us in the community of faith. Worship is grounded in God's command (Matt. 4:10). Our worship here and now anticipates the eternal praise of all God's saints as we "worship the one who lives forever and ever" (Rev. 4:10).

59. Why does the prayer of confession list sins I never commit?

When we say the corporate or unison prayer of confession that is usually a part of Presbyterian worship services, it is a time when the gathered congregation confesses sins that affect all of humanity. The focus of this prayer is often on issues that are much broader than personal sins and are our sins and shortcomings as part of the human family of God. These are dimensions that very often we would overlook in the private confession of our own sins.

So we should not be surprised to be surprised by some of what is confessed in this prayer! The prayer helps us focus on the broader vision of who we are as sinful persons. It points us to our complicities and involvements in structures of sinfulness or attitudes of sin that are pervasive in our world and in our cultures. It draws us out beyond the particular actions we do in personal relationships to the wider web of relationships in which we are involved as persons who live in a particular time and place but whose participation in our cultures can have sinful effects about which we seldom think. So while we may not identify specifically with the sin being confessed, we do recognize our solidarity with other humans as part of the human family, and thus our part in establishing and fostering sinful attitudes or practices.

Presbyterians also see our corporate prayers of confession as ways of praying on behalf of those in the human family who are not aware of their sins and their participation in sinful structures or institutions. So we are praying not only for ourselves but for the whole world. We stand side by side with all people as part of the human race, and we all need God's forgiveness. Our prayers are offered on behalf of others who do not pray, or cannot pray, or will not pray. As Jesus prayed for his disciples (Luke 22:32), for the church (John 17), and even commanded us to pray for enemies (Matt. 5:44), so we in our corporate worship of God pray on behalf of ourselves and all others seeking God's pardon and forgiveness for our sins.

60. Why don't Presbyterian churches have altars?

When you walk into many churches and look to the front you see an altar. In Roman Catholic churches this is a central focus, since in the Mass when the Eucharist is observed the eucharistic elements, the bread and the wine, are placed on the altar, and the priest recites the liturgy in which the elements become the body and blood of Jesus Christ. In the Mass, Jesus Christ is resacrificed for the sins of the world.

Presbyterian churches have a Communion table instead of an altar. We believe that the sacrifice of Jesus Christ has been offered once and for all on the cross (Heb. 7:27; 9:26). In the Lord's Supper, or Communion, we remember that sacrifice, are nourished by it, and receive the benefits of Christ's death for us by faith through the power of the Holy Spirit. We do not believe that the bread and wine "become" the body and blood of Christ in any literal or physical way. The elements are the means by which the gospel message of Jesus Christ comes to us and is received by believers in the context of the Christian community.

So Presbyterian churches have Communion tables instead of

altars. An altar is where a sacrifice is offered. We believe that the sacrifice of Christ has already been definitively offered in his death on the cross. So now we remember that death, appropriate what Christ has done for us, and commit ourselves to Christ's service as we eat and drink together in the sacrament of the Lord's Supper.

We do this from the Communion table, which should be placed on the level of the congregation rather than elevated above the people's level as an altar would be. We receive the Communion elements from the Lord's Table as the common elements of life, which reminds us that Jesus Christ became a human, like us, to bring the salvation that God gives to human sinners.

When elders distribute the Communion elements to the congregation, we are reminded that we receive Jesus Christ from our neighbor and that we communicate Jesus Christ to our neighbors. The Lord's Supper celebrates what God has done in Christ. We do not try to repeat this act from an altar, but rather to commemorate it and receive the benefits of Christ for our lives.

61. Why don't Presbyterian churches have altar calls?

Altar calls became an established part of religious culture in America during the various revival movements that began in the eighteenth and flourished in the nineteenth century. These revivals often took place outside of churches, in camp meetings or tents, and were often led by itinerant evangelists. Revivals featured an altar call at the end of the service, in which the service participants were invited to come forward and to make a public profession of their faith in Jesus Christ. The altar call was linked with the preaching of the evangelist, who preached to bring people to a decision to "accept Christ." Churches in a number of denominations with revivalism in their traditions have continued the practice of an altar call at the end of their worship services.

Presbyterians believe in calling people to have faith in Jesus Christ and foster their public professions of faith. But, in most cases, a service of worship in a Presbyterian church is viewed as a service in which those who have already professed their faith in Christ have gathered together, called by the Holy Spirit of God, to worship God and to celebrate who God is and what God has done. The assumption is that persons are present in response to God's call in Jesus Christ. The service of worship is to praise and glorify God, pray, listen to Scripture, hear God's Word, and respond to God's grace. The church is the gathered community of believers.

Thus, Presbyterians do not have altar calls as regular features of the worship service. There are times and places where people are invited to confess their faith publicly, to be instructed in Christian faith, and to demonstrate their desire to be disciples of Jesus Christ in the church. But Presbyterians do not believe the purpose of every sermon is to elicit initial faith in Christ every time. The preacher is preaching to those who have professed their faith and are gathered as the Christian community. Preaching is to convey God's Word to believers, to build up the community of faith, and to address Christian disciples in the church. Preaching nurtures faith, challenges faith, and leads to further understanding of faith for those who believe and are called together by God's Spirit into the body of Christ.

62. What is preaching, and why is it important?

Preaching is the proclaiming of God's Word. Preaching is the communication of God's will and purposes. Preaching is such a central part of Presbyterian worship because we believe that, through the preaching event, God uses the human words of the preacher to convey a divine message, particularly the message of salvation in Jesus Christ.

For God to be known, God must be revealed. The astonishing claim of the Christian church is that God is and has been revealed in the person of Jesus Christ. We know of Jesus Christ through the Scriptures of the Old and New Testaments. When these Scriptures are proclaimed, explained, and their implications drawn out for contemporary people, we believe God through the Holy Spirit blesses that work and communicates what God wants people of faith in the church to hear. An important confession in our Presbyterian heritage, the Second Helvetic Confession, says: "The Preaching of the Word of God is the Word of God" (*BC* 5.004).

This does not mean that everything that comes out of a preacher's mouth is "guaranteed" to be a word from the Lord! It does mean that when the Scriptures are interpreted, explained, and proclaimed in a faithful and responsible manner, God's word can be heard by people whose hearts and minds are illuminated by the Holy Spirit. The sermon is the form that Christian preaching takes in worship. A sermon may be heard by different people in different ways. This can be regarded as the work of the Holy Spirit, who applies the preached word to the lives and conditions of individual hearers as well as to the gathered church congregation as a whole.

The great figures of the Bible in both the Old and the New Testament were people who proclaimed the message God wanted communicated to the world and to the people of God. Jesus came preaching (Mark 1:38), seeing this as his mission. He sent his disciples to proclaim the message of salvation (Mark 3:14). The amazing thing is that God uses humans—like us—to communicate with the world! Preaching is crucial as our way of hearing God's message in our ever-changing circumstances. Presbyterians see preaching as God's gift to the church, a means by which faith is born (Rom. 10:17) and growth in the Christian faith takes place.

63. Why do Presbyterians insist sacraments be celebrated only in worship services?

We believe the place where baptism and the Lord's Supper are rightly administered is in the service of worship of God's people. Sacraments are celebrated in the context of worship, since they are the gifts of God for the people of God. So, in local circumstances, Presbyterians do not sanction private baptisms or observances of the Lord's Supper apart from worship in the local congregation.

Also, sacraments are to be observed in a service of worship to maintain our theological belief that Word and sacrament belong together. God's word comes to us through the reading of Scripture and its proclamation in preaching. The Word makes clear the meaning of the sacrament. So sacraments should not be administered without the proclamation of the Word. Sacraments are sometimes called the "visible words of God." To make the significance of the sacraments clear, preaching is needed. A right participation in the sacrament is assisted by proclamation of what the sacrament means for the congregation worshiping together. Sacraments are means of personally appropriating the Word that comes to us through preaching. Thus the Lord's Supper should not be observed without being accompanied by preaching. Word and sacrament as bound up together are an important means of God's grace to us. Both are to be found in the service of worship where the people of God are gathered together as the church.

Presbyterians acknowledge there may be times when, due to particular pastoral circumstances, the sacraments may be administered apart from normal congregational worship. These exceptions may be authorized by the church's session. Often, for example, a pastor and an elder (representing the congregation) take the sacrament of the Lord's Supper to church members who for health reasons are not able to be present in the worship service.

But the main perspective in our understandings of worship and sacraments is that baptism and the Lord's Supper are to be observed in the service of worship where the Word of God is read and proclaimed through preaching.

64. What is the relation between worship and the rest of life?

Presbyterian Christians worship God corporately and personally. We gather with the people of God in the church to celebrate God's worth. Here our identity as God's children is confirmed, and we are called to forms of discipleship in mission and ministry to the world. In daily personal worship, we experience God's presence, accept God's grace, and are nurtured in discipleship as we seek to hear God's word and respond through prayer and commitment to serving Jesus Christ in the world.

So the relationship between worship and the rest of our lives is very real and vital. We experience the rhythm of God's grace met by our gratitude, and our gratitude leading to ministries of service. Our service brings us back again to worship. So we move from worship to ministry and from ministry to worship, in an ongoing pattern.

Worship undergirds and forms the context for our ministries. Presbyterian churches live from their worship, as through worship and the sacraments the church is equipped to carry out mission and ministries both within the church body and throughout the world.

Individual Presbyterian Christians are equipped by the means of grace given in worship to carry out personal ministries within the church and throughout the world as well. Among these ministries, supported by the Holy Spirit, are ministries of proclamation and evangelism, compassion, work for peace and justice, caring for creation and life, and witnessing to the reign of God in word and deed. As we participate in these ministries, we are again called to worship, both corporately and personally.

So there is an integral, symbiotic relationship between our worship and the rest of our lives. Without the nourishment and nurture of worship, Presbyterians would experience a power failure of the spirit, a loss of our "lifeline"—our relationship with God. Without being able to praise and honor God with our whole selves in worship, our work in this world would lack vision and power. Worship leads to service and back again to worship. We join with all saints in proclaiming:

> Amen! Blessing and glory and wisdom
> and thanksgiving and honor
> and power and might
> be to our God forever and ever! Amen.
> (Rev. 7:12)

10

Sacraments

65. Why do Presbyterians have two sacraments?

Presbyterian churches recognize two sacraments, baptism and the Lord's Supper. This is in common with many other Protestant churches. In contrast, the Roman Catholic Church has historically recognized seven sacraments: baptism, confirmation, marriage, ordination (holy orders), reconciliation (penance), Eucharist (Lord's Supper), and last rites (extreme unction). During the early history of the church the number of sacraments the church recognized varied. The Roman Catholic tradition has been held to seven since the fifteenth century.

Why these differences?

Presbyterians, and Protestants who recognize sacraments, believe sacraments are God's gracious gifts given by Jesus Christ to the church to establish and nurture faith. We believe the church's sacraments should be available to all persons in the church. These two criteria have been the determining ones for us. A sacrament must have been instituted by Jesus—to have his authority and his command to sanction it; and it must be open and available to all—since all Christians in the church need the sacrament's nourishment. Protestants have questioned the validity of some of the traditional seven sacraments' having been instituted by Jesus, but even more, not all the seven (marriage and ordination, for example) are ones in which everyone can share.

Jesus commanded his disciples to baptize and extend baptism to others (Matt. 28:19; Mark 16:15–16). Jesus commanded his followers to eat and drink together in a commemorative meal for his sacrificial death (Matt. 26:26–29; Mark 14:22–25; Luke 22:14–20; 1 Cor. 10:16; 11:23–26). The signs in these sacraments are the water in baptism and the bread and wine in the Lord's Supper. These are received in faith. In baptism, believers are brought into and incorporated into the church as the community of faith. The community celebrates the Lord's Supper, through which faith is nourished and sustained.

These two sacraments, instituted by Jesus, are for all believers. They are the regular practices of the church. Presbyterians celebrate two sacraments and receive them in gratitude as God's ways of reaching out to us and drawing us into union with Jesus Christ.

66. Why are sacraments important?

Sacraments are God's gifts given to nurture our faith. They are symbolic, in that when we see sacraments celebrated we know that something more than physical activity is occurring. Something significant is happening.

Sacraments are often said to be "visible signs of an invisible grace." They point to a theological reality. They are "signs" and "seals" of that reality. Presbyterians believe sacraments are God's ways of reaching out to us in a visible way to convey God's word, just as God also reaches out to us through hearing as God's Word is preached and proclaimed. Sacraments are the "visible words of God."

Baptism and the Lord's Supper are signs of God's covenant or special relationship with us. They portray before our eyes the benefits that Jesus Christ has given to us. In his life, death, resurrection, and ascension, Christ has given us the gift of salvation. Persons of faith in the church are strengthened in their faith when we see the signs of this salvation enacted in worship.

Baptism and the Lord's Supper are also seals of God's covenant with us in Christ. When we participate in the sacraments by faith, the benefits of Christ's salvation for us are "sealed" in our hearts and minds by the power of the Holy Spirit. They become real to us, meaningful to us, and nurture us whenever we participate in the sacraments. The Holy Spirit makes salvation real and effective to us as our faith is nurtured in the sacraments.

So sacraments are very important parts of our Christian lives in the church. They are God's gracious gifts to give us reminders of our salvation in Christ and also to make that salvation effective to us by the Holy Spirit. When we see the elements of the sacraments—water in baptism, the bread and the wine in the Lord's Supper—the words of the gospel should ring in our ears!

67. Why do Presbyterians baptize babies?

Presbyterians, like many other Protestants and also Roman Catholics, practice infant baptism. Infants are presented by their parents, in a church service, to receive the sacrament of baptism. At that time, parents make vows, as does the congregation.

We baptize babies because we believe our children are included in God's covenant of grace with Christian believers. In the Old Testament, the sign of God's covenant relationship with the people of Israel was circumcision (Gen. 17:11). The New Testament church saw baptism as the new sign of God's covenant with the church, the new people of God (Col. 2:11–15). Jesus Christ is God's "new covenant" (Luke 22:20; 1 Cor. 11:25). In him, all the promises of God find their "Yes" (2 Cor. 1:20). Baptism is a sign of the believer's incorporation into Christ as we are adopted into the family of God.

We also believe that just as in the Old Testament the sign of God's covenant was given to those of faith and their children, so also now the benefits of Jesus Christ as God's new covenant of grace are extended to believers and their children as well (Acts 2:39). In the baptism of infants we recognize this covenant and celebrate the entry of our children into the church. Infant baptism is the sign and seal of God's promises in Jesus Christ to our children.

Traditionally, those baptized as infants are "confirmed" in their faith when they reach an "age of accountability." At that point, young persons affirm the vows taken on their behalf by their parents when they were baptized. In baptism, parents promise to raise their child by teaching faith. The congregation promises to support, nurture, and provide opportunities for the child to grow in faith.

Infant baptism is not a "guarantee" of salvation. But it is a wonderful sign of God's electing love. The helpless child is drawn into the family of God, just as all of us—as sinners—are saved by God's grace "while we [are] weak" and unable to save ourselves (Rom. 5:6).

68. I do not remember my baptism as an infant. Can I be rebaptized?

Presbyterians, with other Christians, do not believe a person should be rebaptized. When a valid baptism is administered in a Christian church, we believe it has efficacy when faith in Jesus Christ is present. This effect is lifelong and, in infant baptism, does not depend on one's remembering the event.

A "valid baptism" in the Christian church has been considered to be one administered in the name of the Father, Son, and Holy Spirit (Matt. 28:19). It is assumed that the person administering the baptism is a person recognized as one who can carry out this function. Baptism is celebrated in the context of the worshiping community of faith. It is celebrated as a sacrament, in the midst of worship where the Word of God is read and proclaimed.

Infants do not generally remember their baptism. Yet the effects and significance of baptism are real and enduring. In the rite of confirmation those who are baptized confirm their own, personal faith and assent to the faith confessed by their parents who brought them for baptism as infants. This confirmation may take place in the teenage years, or later.

The fact that baptism is administered by the church in the context of faith is what gives infant baptism its efficacy. Rebaptism has not been permitted in Christian communities because the nature of baptism is that it is administered once. Later, as people grow into or grow in their faith, their baptism can take on deeper, richer meanings. They do not need a rebaptism, but instead a rededication and recommitment of their lives to what the promises of baptism signify. Some churches in the Baptist traditions require adult baptism by immersion, even for those who have been baptized as infants. This is not to "rebaptize," but because in the Baptist view the infant baptism was not a valid baptism. Adult baptism by immersion is for them the only valid way for baptism to take place. So their requirement is for a "genuine" baptism—of adults—and not a second baptism for new Christian believers. Presbyterians, however, share the view of the ecumenical church that baptism is to be administered only once, and that infants who are baptized spend their lives "living out" the faith expressed by their parents at their baptism and appropriating that faith personally, for themselves, as they mature.

69. What happens in the Lord's Supper?

The Lord's Supper is God's gracious gift of a sacrament to nourish our faith. Baptism marks our entrance into the Christian family. The Lord's Supper is our means of being nourished or sustained in our lives as Christ's disciples. The Supper was instituted by Jesus (1 Cor. 11:23–26). It is a sign and seal of God's grace repeatedly given to us, as often as we celebrate it to communicate the benefits of Christ's death to us, by faith. When we participate in the Lord's Supper the reality of the salvation Christ brings becomes ours.

Presbyterians believe that in the Lord's Supper we experience a fullness of time in which past, present, and future come together.

Past. Jesus commands, "Do this in remembrance of me" (1 Cor. 11:24). Our Supper celebrations look back to Jesus' life, death, and resurrection as the events that have decisively shaped our lives by bringing us salvation. In the Supper, our faith is nourished by our union with Christ, and we are fed by the "bread of life," who brings us eternal life as "the living bread that came down from heaven" (John 6:22–51).

Present. Jesus proclaims, "This cup is the new covenant in my blood" (1 Cor. 11:25). In the Lord's Supper we celebrate the renewal of God's covenant in the person of Jesus Christ. All God's covenant promises, throughout the Old Testament, are fulfilled in Christ who is the "Yes" to all God's promises (2 Cor. 1:20). Jesus is forever present with us. Jesus is present in the Lord's Supper, conveying in himself all that God will be and do for us as God's people.

Future. We celebrate the Lord's Supper remembering, as we do, that we "proclaim the Lord's death until he comes" (1 Cor. 11:26). We anticipate the great messianic banquet of the future kingdom of God (Matt. 8:11; Mark 14:25; Luke 22:18), a joyful meal of happiness with God, with Christ as the host and the saints of all ages gathered together. Then the future reign of God's kingdom will be celebrated with thanksgiving in eternal joy.

More "happens" in the Lord's Supper than we can ever realize. Presbyterians join other Christians around the Lord's Table to rejoice in salvation and to eat and drink with Jesus and with one another. We gather to celebrate the joyful feast of the people of God!

70. Do we really eat and drink the "body and blood" of Jesus in the Lord's Supper?

When early Christians celebrated the Lord's Supper, remembering Jesus' words as he spoke of the bread and the cup being his body and blood (Luke 22:19–20; 1 Cor. 11:23–26), some outside the church thought Christians were cannibals. It sounded as though the Lord's Supper was a cannibalistic ritual involving flesh and blood.

The primary Presbyterian belief is that "body and blood" here refer to the death of Jesus. By eating and drinking in the Lord's Supper we are receiving the benefits of what Christ's death on the cross has brought us. The purpose of the Supper is to enable us to remember and receive the great gift of salvation that Jesus' death makes possible for us. Jesus said, "This is my body that is for you" (1 Cor. 11:24) and "This cup that is poured out for you is the new covenant in my blood" (Luke 22:20). Jesus died for us (Rom. 5:8). The Lord's Supper is a way of nourishing and strengthening our faith, to assure us that God is faithful in all God's covenant promises, and especially in the "new covenant," who is Jesus Christ himself (1 Cor. 11:25; Jer. 31:31–34). The elements in the Lord's Supper, the bread and the wine, represent the body and blood of Christ in a symbolic way. They "represent," and they also "present," Christ to us so that by participating in faith, we abide in Christ and Christ in us. We eat and drink unto "eternal life" (John 6:54–56).

Presbyterians do not believe the "substance" of the bread and wine are changed into the body and blood of Christ, the view of the Roman Catholic Church known as transubstantiation. We believe Jesus Christ is present with us in the Supper, by faith through the power of the Holy Spirit, even though he is ascended into heaven and "sitteth on the right hand of God the Father Almighty" (Apostles' Creed). Jesus Christ and his benefits are communicated to us in the Supper, through the power of the Holy Spirit, as we are united with Christ by faith.

We receive Jesus Christ in gratitude, realizing that the Supper is God's gracious gift, reaching out to convey salvation and to nourish our faith. We celebrate the Lord's Supper with glad and joyful hearts as we "proclaim the Lord's death until he comes" (1 Cor. 11:26).

71. Can unconfirmed children and nonchurch members take Communion?

Some Presbyterian church bodies permit baptized children to participate in the Lord's Supper. Others require that only confirmed children are allowed to partake of the Supper. Presbyterian churches do not require that those who participate in the Supper be members of the church where the worship service is held, or even of a Presbyterian church. We recognize the Lord's Supper is for all Christians, and those who have faith in Jesus Christ are welcomed at his Table.

Presbyterian churches that do not permit baptized children to participate in the Lord's Supper until they are confirmed or have "joined the church" stress that faith in Jesus Christ must be informed by knowledge and that those who participate in the Supper should understand what they are doing and what the sacrament means. Thus, they should have instruction in the church's doctrine so they can participate in the sacrament intelligently and meaningfully.

Presbyterian churches that permit baptized children who are yet unconfirmed or have not "joined the church" to participate in the Lord's Supper stress that faith is not only an intellectual understanding but is fundamentally an attitude of trust. Children can trust in Jesus Christ. Though many may not have as full an intellectual understanding as some adults, faith is not measured by "how much" knowledge one has. Jesus commanded "little children" to come to him (Luke 18:16), and where better can they "come" to him than in the Supper?

Some Reformed churches in eighteenth-century New England saw the sacraments as "converting ordinances." They argued that even if persons who did not have faith in Christ participated, they might gain faith through the sacrament. Others have argued that the Lord's Supper is a meal celebrating what Christ has done for all people, so all people should be invited to participate in this joyful feast.

Most Presbyterian churches, however, issue an invitation to the Lord's Supper to those who have faith in Christ and have been baptized. The sacrament is a nourishing of faith for those who share a common confession of Christ as Lord and Savior. It is the gift of God for the people of God. Thus, the only requirement for participating is commitment of faith which is expressed through the sign of baptism.

11

Christian Life

72. What do Presbyterians believe about saints?

Presbyterians believe that saints are Christians and that Christians are saints.

The word "saint" means one who is "set apart," "separate," or "holy." In the New Testament, it is a common term to refer to Christians in local churches (Col. 1:2; Eph. 1:1; Phil. 1:1). The saints are those who are "God's beloved" and are "called to be saints" (Rom. 1:7; 1 Cor. 1:2).

The sixteenth-century Protestant Reformers reacted strongly against what they believed was a mistaken view of saints by the Roman Catholic Church. There the emphasis was on the lives of saints, their special "holiness," and also the view that saints who have died can play a role in the lives of the living on earth. Reformation confessions admonished that saints are not to be adored, worshiped, or invoked (see the Second Helvetic Confession, *BC* 5.025). The Reformers were afraid people viewed saints as their mediators with God, or bestowed on them the honor of worship or the power to intercede with God when one prays. These functions, the Reformers believed, are not ascribed to "saints" in the New Testament. They also usurp the place of Jesus Christ, who is the "one mediator between God and humankind" (1 Tim. 2:5), and introduce another rival "god" if a saint is "worshiped." The Reformers believed that it is only the Holy Spirit and Jesus Christ who intercede with God on our behalf in prayer (Rom. 8:26, 27, 34; Heb. 7:25).

Presbyterians see all Christians as "saints," not because they are especially "holy" or "perfect" or never sin. All Christians, while saved by the work of Jesus Christ, are still sinners in constant need of God's forgiveness in Christ. The church is the "communion of saints" (Apostles' Creed). One way to understand this phrase is to see it as referring to the church as the fellowship of Christians— all the "saints." A wider view is to have a comprehensive view of the church and to realize that the church on earth is surrounded by a "great . . . cloud of witnesses" (Heb. 12:11)—all the saints who have died and are now in heaven. Their lives and witness can inspire us and be powerful examples or models to help us live our Christian lives.

73. Do Presbyterians believe that Christians can attain perfection in this life?

No. Historically Presbyterians have not believed Christians can be "perfect" in this life.

We recognize that Christians are forgiven sinners. We are for-given by God through the work of Jesus Christ. But even as Chris-tians, we continue to sin during our days on earth. This is why we need to ask for God's forgiveness daily. We confess our sins cor-porately and individually in worship services on Sunday morn-ings. Though we have been given the gift of salvation and peace with God through our Lord Jesus Christ (Rom. 5:1), Christians are still sinners. Martin Luther expressed this by saying that the Chris-tian is "at the same time just [saved] and a sinner."

Christians in the Methodist tradition, which goes back to John Wesley (1703–91), have traditionally believed in "Christian per-fection." Christians will do good works as a result of their salva-tion, obey God's law, and attain a perfection of love that will be a prior step into God's presence in Christ. Christians will not act contrary to pure love.

Presbyterians, however, believe that Christians can and do grow in God's grace as we become conformed to the image of Christ (Rom. 8:29), but that we do not attain perfection during this life.

Even as Christians, the power of sin will still be a reality in our lives that will taint and affect our motives and actions. We can never be "pure" or "perfect" in any way by God's standards. Our perfection comes with our "glorification," which is our eternal life in heaven with God. It is only then that we will attain the fullness of any type of perfection.

For Presbyterians, the Christian life forms a zigzag pattern. We grow in God's grace, obeying God's law and will out of gratitude for the wonderful gift of salvation given to us in Jesus Christ—we "zig." But we still sin. We may fall into habits of sin for a period of time, and sin may seem to have a hold on us—we "zag." But through it all, by the power of God's Holy Spirit in our lives, we are growing in our faith, even at times when that growth is painful. So we rely on God's ongoing forgiveness as we confess our sin. We look forward to the perfection of heaven in the presence of God.

74. If we are Christians, do we have to obey God's law?

If we are Christians, we will want to obey God's law.

Christians are persons who are saved by faith in Jesus Christ. It is not our good works that save us, but solely our faith in Jesus Christ as God's Son, our Lord and Savior (Gal. 2:16; Phil. 3:9). It is in Christ that we receive forgiveness for our sins and are reconciled with God (2 Cor. 5:16–21), so that we can have peace (Rom. 5:1).

It is because of this experience of salvation that we desire to follow God's law in our Christian lives. Presbyterians believe that God's moral law is expressed in the Ten Commandments. This is distinct from the ceremonial laws of the Old Testament, which are now not binding on Christians. We no longer offer animal sacrifices to God, since Jesus Christ has died on the cross as the once, final sacrifice for sin (Heb. 9:26; 10:12).

God's moral law is the expression of God's will. It is God's way of telling people how God wants them to live—in relation to God and in relation to one another. This was why God gave the Ten Commandments to the people of Israel (Ex. 20:1). God's law is seen in the Old Testament as the good gift which is to be loved and in which there is delight (Ps. 119:77, 97, 174).

Presbyterians have always emphasized that we obey God's law now, as Christians, as a way of showing our gratitude for God's grace in Jesus Christ. We do not obey God's law *in order to gain* salvation; we obey God's law *as an expression of* salvation. There is a huge difference between these two approaches. The law instructs us on the "shape" our Christian lives should take. It shows us the concern God has for how we live and the practical ways we should live in order to obey God's will. The law is a great gift because it conveys to us the desires of God. John Calvin called this the "principal use" of the law. Our Christian lives move from faith to further understanding. The law of God helps us understand God's will and purposes for us.

So we obey God's law out of the overwhelming gratitude we have for God's loving, electing grace expressed to us in Jesus Christ. We move from Grace to Gratitude to Obedience.

75. Does God answer prayer?

Yes. Presbyterians believe God answers prayer. We believe it because the Bible from cover to cover provides us with many examples, and also because we, like countless Christians who have gone before us, have experienced God's answers to our prayers in our own lives.

If Jesus was who we believe he was—truly divine and truly human—it is significant that Jesus practiced prayer constantly and urged his followers to do the same (Luke 11:2), even giving us the Lord's Prayer as a model for our own (Matt. 6:9–15). God invites us to call upon the Lord, even in the day of trouble (Ps. 50:15).

So we are commanded to pray. We can also expect God to answer our prayers according to the divine will, a truth that is affirmed in all four Gospels (Matt. 21:22; Mark 11:24; Luke 11:9;

John 11:22). When we seek to pray according to God's will we are giving ourselves over to being open to what God desires and trying to align ourselves with God's purposes. This was the prayer of Jesus in the Garden of Gethsemane: "Not my will but yours be done" (Luke 22:42).

How does God answer prayer? God answers through many means. We often hear it said that God may answer our prayers in three ways: yes, no, or not yet. This affirms that every prayer has an "answer." The answer may not be what we want or expect or what we think is best. But the essence of prayer is trust. When we perceive God's answers to our prayers, our goal should be to trust those answers as being what is best for us. Just as we trust God to hear our prayers and to answer, so we should trust those answers we receive, even when they seem difficult or hard for us to follow.

Prayer should be a tremendously exciting element of our Christian lives. God is with us, God cares for us, God guides us, God loves us. These affirmations mean that as we pray and seek God's will for our lives and our situations, we can trust God's answers and believe that we are being led in the paths God desires. In prayer, we can "expect the unexpected." We never know how, when, or where God will answer our prayers. And that's exciting!

76. Does God heal today?

We often hear very meaningful stories of people who believe God has healed them. Sometimes these are experiences where doctors appear to have no medical explanations for how health has returned. At other times people attribute their healings to God when they believe God has worked through medical science or those who have cared for them.

We also occasionally hear of persons who claim to be "faith healers." They are often itinerant ministers who hold healing services in different places, and at times often dramatic results appear to occur. These faith healers proclaim that if people only "have faith," they can be healed.

Theologically, we cannot say that if we simply "have faith," some automatic results for healing will occur. This would be emphasizing our human abilities to "have faith" and also would be putting us in the position of saying to God: "I have faith, therefore you must heal me!" So the term "faith healing" can be problematic if it is used with these assumptions underlying it.

Presbyterians recognize that a better phrase is "divine healing." It is important to recognize, theologically, that all healing comes as a result of God's action. It is God who is the giver of health. Jesus did miracles of healing. Later apostles attributed powers to heal with the "name" or authority of Jesus Christ (Acts 3:16; 4:10). Sometimes God may work dramatically in situations where no known human "remedy" can account for healing. Most often, God works to bring health and wholeness through those who practice the healing arts. It is perfectly appropriate to attribute our healing to God who uses those persons who are gifted with medical knowledge and expertise.

At times, we pray for healing and none appears to come. This is not a reflection on the inadequacy of our faith. Instead, we should continue to pray and trust God for the best resolution to the need. There are many kinds of healing beyond the physical or medical. When we see the healing of relationships in families, among peoples, or of enemies, we realize that God's healing powers are at work in these experiences. There again, God may use people to be the means of bringing about reconciliation and peace.

77. How do we know the will of God?

Clearly, Christians are to live our earthly lives "no longer by human desires but by the will of God" (1 Pet. 4:2). This was Jesus' supreme desire, "to do the will of him who sent me" (John 4:34; Luke 22:42). When we do the will of God, we are Jesus' own "brother and sister and mother" (Mark 3:35). The mark of the faithful Israelite is to delight in doing God's will (Ps. 40:8).

Yet knowing the will of God for us, as a church or as individuals, is not always easy. Sometimes our choices are quite clear, since the options are clear-cut. Other times, there are baffling perplexities and paralyzing ambiguities. Several guides can help.

Presbyterians will always turn first to the two primary means through which God communicates with us: Scripture and prayer. We will seek God's guidance for our decisions by reading God's Word and by praying. We desire to be taught to do God's will (Ps. 143:10) as we try to discern and understand it. God's law is an aid in this endeavor. Through prayer, God leads us.

Relatedly, we will share our struggles about the will of God with the community of faith. God's Spirit is active in the body of Christ, and insights of other Christians are helpful in leading us to understand what God may be telling us to be or do in our circumstances. One of the blessings of being part of the fellowship of faith is to gain from the perspectives shared by other church members.

More specifically, we should recognize that God's will is focused most clearly for us in the person of Jesus Christ. Our questions should lead us to ask, not so much "What would Jesus do?" as "What would Jesus have me do?" Is what I wish to do like Jesus himself? Can I understand this action to be in harmony with what Jesus taught? Does it further Jesus' ministry? Is it consistent with the values Jesus embodied in his life?

We pose these questions and then we make our decision in faith. We trust God to guide us, even if an individual decision does not turn out to be the best decision it could have been. We trust God's continuing love and Spirit, believing that "those who do the will of God live forever" (1 John 2:17).

78. What is my Christian "vocation"?

"Vocation" means "calling." When we speak of our "Christian vocation" we refer to our calling to be disciples of Jesus Christ. Jesus "called" his disciples (Mark 1:20; Luke 6:13). Paul writes that God "calls" people to salvation (Rom. 8:30) and into the "fellowship of his Son, Jesus Christ" (1 Cor. 1:9). So, first and foremost, according to the New Testament, our "calling" is to be Christians. Like the disciples, we "follow" our Master. This is a way of describing Christian salvation. God calls us in Christ, we respond in faith, and receive hope (Eph. 1:18; 4:4).

The Protestant reformers Martin Luther and John Calvin both extended the idea of "vocation" or "calling" to include not only our salvation, but also our service to God in Christ in this world. In the Roman Catholic Church in the sixteenth century, it was only the "religious"—the priests or monks or nuns—who were considered to have a "vocation." But the Reformers believed the New Testament indicates that all who respond in faith as disciples of Jesus Christ have a "calling" to live out their salvation by serving God, through who they are and what they do. Calvin stressed that our "calling" is the basis for our life's actions. God calls us to our jobs, our ministries, our forms of service as "sentry posts" to keep our lives from being topsy-turvy. Our duties in serving God give us purpose and stability for our lives as Christians. Our occupations or professions are ways of serving, and should be viewed as the "calling" through which we live out our Christian discipleship. What we do in serving Christ—as a parent, or caregiver, or volunteer, or professional person—these are our "callings," our "vocation." We serve Christ in these ways, just as those who carry out ordained offices in the church also serve Christ. Both "clergy" and "laity" have a vocation—to be Christian in all we do, in service to this world.

So Presbyterians recognize that if all Christians could see their work and service as their "callings," a strong sense of renewal and "reformation" would energize our churches. What we do during a week is not irrelevant or unimportant. It is our vocation, our calling, and is the way we live out our discipleship as followers of Jesus Christ. God calls us, and we respond in faith and service.

12

Reign of God

79. Why is our view of the future important?

Our views about the future and what God is doing in the days to come are very important to us. This is because our views of the future shape our lives in the present.

Usually we think it is our view of the past—of history—that shapes us, our understandings, and our actions. Certainly this is true to some degree.

But it is also our view of the future that pulls us forward. If we did not believe there was a reason to hope, a reason to live for tomorrow—then we wouldn't get out of bed today! We need a hope that draws us into God's future to provide the meaning and significance we need for our daily lives, and to give us the peace and joy we need to face our own deaths and beyond.

Presbyterians share the Christian conviction that in the resurrection of Jesus Christ, God's future has, in a sense, already occurred. The resurrection of Christ is the assurance of our own resurrections (1 Cor. 15:51–58), for "we will certainly be united with him in a resurrection like his"(Rom. 6:5). The resurrection of Christ means the defeat of evil and sin and death and all enemies of God (Col. 2:15; 1 Cor. 15:25, 27; Eph. 1:22). So we can believe that the future is secure. God in Christ has triumphed over every power that can hurt or destroy us. The reign of God is taking shape in history and beyond history. In the resurrection, we see God's power to raise Jesus Christ (Rom. 6:4). We believe that same power is at work today through the Holy Spirit and will bring to pass God's final, ultimate reign, for which we pray: "Your kingdom come" (Luke 11:2).

This is the Christian hope. It is hope for the future, grounded in God's past action in raising Jesus Christ, that enables us to live and serve and endure all that we face in the present. Christ Jesus is our hope (1 Tim. 1:1). So our view of the future and the assurances we have enable us to live our Christian lives in freedom, boldness, peace, and joy. We believe that God is with us in Christ by the Holy Spirit, both now and forever. This is the greatest comfort and the greatest challenge we can receive. We who "set our hope on Christ" can also now "live for the praise of his glory" (Eph. 1:12).

80. What do we believe about the end of the world?

Presbyterians have varying beliefs about the end of the world. This is because the Bible says a number of things about the future that have been variously interpreted. If you go into a bookstore and see a whole shelf of books that claim to present the "biblical" view of the end of the world, you'll find that each one construes what will happen and when a little differently! These writers should realize the Bible does not intend to give us a detailed blueprint about when the world will end, or a sequence of events that will follow one after another. Instead, the Bible wants to convey theological convictions to provide us with all we need for facing the future.

All Christians affirm in the Apostles' Creed that we believe Jesus Christ "will come again to judge the quick [living] and the dead." This is the next event on the divine timetable. Jesus Christ will return to earth. The New Testament pictures of the events that follow vary. Some are portrayed in vivid, apocalyptic imagery—such as in the book of Revelation.

We do believe that the end of the world ("eschatology" is the study of the "end things") will initiate certain events that belong to God's ultimate reign, or kingdom. The Scriptures describe a last judgment (Matt. 25:31–46), a resurrection of the body (1 Cor. 15), and eternal life lived in the presence of God, when God is "all in all" (Eph. 1:23). God's judgment on evil and wickedness will be real, and the images of a "lake of fire" into which "the devil," "Death," and "Hades" are cast (Rev. 19:20; 20:10, 14, 15) are dramatic ways of establishing that God's purposes and reign will be total and complete, overcoming all sin (Rev. 21:27), and that all things will ultimately be reconciled to God (Col. 1:20).

The end of this world is the prelude to God's establishing "a new heaven and a new earth" (Rev. 21:1) marked by God's eternal presence and peace. This is the Christian hope and this is the Christian assurance. This is why Christians pray, "Come, Lord Jesus!" (Rev. 22:20).

81. When will Jesus come again?

We don't know when the return of Jesus Christ will take place. This was what Jesus himself taught when he said, "But about that day and hour no one knows, neither the angels of heaven, nor the Son, but only the Father" (Matt. 24:36). Speculation beyond this is fruitless. Yet there are some things we can say.

We believe that the return of Jesus is certain. Jesus promised his return when he told his disciples, "And if I go and prepare a place for you, I will come again and will take you to myself, so that where I am, there you may be also" (John 14:3). We affirm in the Apostles' Creed that Jesus will "come again." Christians call this "the blessed hope" (Titus 2:13).

We also believe that it is impossible to ascertain or predict when the return of Jesus will take place. Some Christians make the return of Jesus a very central aspect of their faith, so much so that it seems nearly the only focus of their Christian experience. These are people who may be said to have an "eschatological itch!" Eschatology is the study of the "end times," the conclusion of history. To have an "eschatological itch" is to make the future such a focal point for faith that other aspects of Jesus' teachings and ministry are neglected. We still hear of groups who are persuaded by a charismatic leader that Jesus will return at a certain day or hour. In 1843, a group following William Miller sold all their possessions and waited for the return of Jesus on a hillside in New York. Jesus did not return.

A more balanced view is what Presbyterians have typically adopted. We recognize the reality of Jesus' coming again, but as we anticipate it we "keep awake" (Matt. 25:13) and "watch" (Mark 13:32–37). This means we continue to be vigorous in the work of mission and ministry that Jesus has entrusted to the church. Our time of waiting for Jesus' return during our "slice of history" is to be marked by our service to Christ.

We can say this. The return of Jesus is always "imminent"—it can happen at any time. But it may not be "immediate." There may be many more centuries of history before Jesus returns. Yet this much is certain too: the return of Jesus is closer now than it was when you began to read this answer!

82. Do Presbyterians have to worry about being "left behind"?

A recent, popular set of books and movies portray the return of Jesus Christ to earth to gather up true Christians into the air with him, while leaving behind those who are not true believers in Christ. This scenario is presumably based on 1 Thessalonians 4:13–18. A term that has also been associated with this passage is the "rapture." Sometimes one even sees a bumper sticker that says: "In case of rapture, this car will be driverless"!

The effect of this interpretation relating to the return of Christ leaves many people uneasy or even scared. An implication is that if you do not truly believe in Christ, you will be "left behind" at Christ's return to face the evil of the world and all that will follow in terms of God's justice and judgment, leading to eternal death in hell.

This approach is dramatically different from the positive view of Jesus' return as a "blessed hope" (Titus 2:13) and as the beginning of the fullness of God's glorious reign, for which we pray in the Lord's Prayer: "Your kingdom come" (Matt. 6:10). Presbyterians can best adopt this biblical perspective!

The future and the return of Christ, the establishment of God's reign, the events of the future life are all to be greeted with hope and expectation, according to the New Testament. Presbyterians believe that as we are elected and called by God, given the gift of faith, and drawn by the Holy Spirit into the church, we have the confidence of the children of God (2 Cor. 3:4; 5:8). We look forward to the return of Jesus, for "when he is revealed, we will be like him, for we will see him as he is" (1 John 3:2). This should not leave us uneasy and scared but, rather, joyfully anticipating the future! We should never fear being "left behind." Biblical scholars debate exactly what the passage in 1 Thessalonians is intended to mean. But the dominant note for the future is that Presbyterian Christians can be joyful in the Lord, believing our salvation is secure in Jesus Christ, and trusting in the hope in which we are saved (Rom. 8:24).

83. What do Presbyterians believe about the "millennium"?

There have been three main views about "millenarianism," and one can find Presbyterians who have believed each of these three views.

The term "millenarianism" comes from a reference to a "thousand-year" reign of Christ in Revelation 20:1–10. This is also called "chiliasm" from the Greek term *chilioi* (or *chilias*) meaning "thousand." The three main views about what the thousand-year reign of Christ means began in the early church as Christians pondered the future and the return, or second coming, of Jesus Christ.

"Premillennialism" is the view that Christ will return to earth before his thousand-year reign begins. His coming is prior to, or "pre-," millennial. The thousand-year reign is interpreted literally as the period when Jesus will be physically present on earth and rule over all nations. Premillennialists stress the importance of evangelism and being ready for Jesus' return at any time.

"Postmillennialism" is the view that Jesus' second coming to earth will occur after a special earthly reign of one thousand years. His second coming is "post-" or "after" his millennial rule. The rule is marked by a spread of the gospel, its reception by many people, and a fighting against evil. Postmillennialists stress the role humans can play in establishing a better world here and now.

"Amillennialism" is the view that the "thousand year" image should not be interpreted literally, but is a figurative description for Christ's rule and reign in the church and through history. This view originated with St. Augustine in the fourth century. It emphasizes the church's continuing struggle against evil and the need to proclaim the gospel to every person. This view has probably been the majority view of most Presbyterians.

Since no one millennial view has been the "only" Presbyterian position, we realize that this is a question on which Presbyterians as well as other Christians will vary. One opinion should never be absolutized and made a requirement for belief, as is done in some Christian bodies.

84. What is the "resurrection of the body"?

We affirm in the Apostles' Creed that we believe in "the resurrection of the body." This is a statement of our faith about the future and about God's power in our lives both now and forever.

At death, our physical bodies cease functioning. They return to the earth, "ashes to ashes and dust to dust." But, as Christians, we believe that physical death is not the end to our existence. Death is not a period at the end of our life's sentence, it is a colon that leads to the life to come, or the fullness of eternal life.

Presbyterians believe in the resurrection of the body as God's act of raising us up, after our physical death, and giving us a spiritual body that enables us to live eternal life in God's presence. The "resurrection body" of which Paul writes in 1 Cor. 15:35–58 is the imperishable body which is ours because Jesus Christ is raised from the dead. The dead will be resurrected (1 Cor. 15:12–34).

Christ is the "first fruits of those who have died" (1 Cor. 15:20). We who die physically after Christ are raised with a "spiritual body" (1 Cor. 15:44), or resurrection body, which is imperishable, immortal (1 Cor. 15:52–55), and in which the joys of eternal life are experienced. Our mortal bodies in themselves are not capable of living in the full presence of the eternal God. Our spiritual bodies can experience the true spiritual communion with the Lord and with the saints that is expressed in praise to God by the "great multitude in heaven" (Rev. 19:1–10).

We cannot know or comprehend what our resurrection body will be like. We know from Jesus' appearance after his resurrection that he was capable of going through locked doors (John 20:19) as well as cooking breakfast for his disciples (John 21:12). We will, presumably, recognize others in heaven. Our bodies will not be the limitation they are now to experiencing the fullness of fellowship and love which finds its ultimate fulfillment in our praise of the eternal God.

85. What is the kingdom of God?

The kingdom of God, or reign of God, means God's ultimate rule over all creation. In the Bible, images of God as "king" or "reigning" are used to point to the belief that God's will and purposes will be established and last forever. This was a vision found throughout the Old Testament and was fueled by the Hebrew prophets, who anticipated a coming "day of the LORD" when God would judge the world (Amos 5:18–20; Zeph. 1:14–18), as a prelude to the final kingdom where God's rule will establish peace and justice (Isa. 2:2–4; Mic. 4:1–4). The coming of the Messiah will mark the establishment of the "age to come" as a radical break from the "present age" (as anticipated in Isa. 11; cf. Mark 10:30).

Jesus' central message was that the kingdom of God has begun with his coming and the proclamation of the "good news" (Mark 1:15; Luke 4:43) in his ministry as he preached, healed, forgave, and embodied God's love. At the same time, Jesus taught his disciples to pray for and anticipate the time of fulfillment when God's reign will be finally established: "Your kingdom come. Your will be done, on earth as it is in heaven" (Matt. 6:10; Luke 11:2). God's reign has already come in Jesus, but it has not yet arrived in its final form.

Presbyterians believe we live in this period between the "already" and the "not yet." We serve Jesus Christ in the church, sharing the good news of the gospel and serving the world in ministries of compassion, justice, and peace. In these actions, we have an anticipation of God's ultimate reign. We get a small "preview" of the coming kingdom.

Yet, we also believe the fullness of the future kingdom will come through God's actions in establishing it. There will come a day when God's final future will be revealed. Then all God's purposes in history and beyond will be realized completely and eternally. God's triumph over all resistance, evil, and sin will be accomplished. This will be the day when "at the name of Jesus / every knee should bend, / in heaven and on earth and under the earth, / and every tongue should confess / that Jesus Christ is Lord, / to the glory of God the Father" (Phil. 2:10–11). Then, "the kingdom of the world has become the kingdom of our Lord / and of his Messiah, / and he will reign forever and ever" (Rev. 11:15).

13

Polity

86. What are the main features of the Presbyterian form of church government?

There are three basic forms of government found among churches. A hierarchical or episcopal form is marked by power lodged in the office of bishop. The bishop exercises authority over churches from that office. This form of government is found in the Roman Catholic Church, Episcopal churches, and Methodist churches.

The second type of church government is the congregational form. Here, the church is the congregation. Each acts autonomously and independently of other groups. In denominations with congregational forms of government, churches may join together in a federation or seek guidance from a larger grouping of churches. But ultimate decision making rests in the local congregation. The United Church of Christ and various Congregational denominations, as well as Baptist churches, are examples of the congregational form of church government.

The Presbyterian form of government is representational. Local congregations elect a group of elders called a session for oversight. Representatives of sessions and the clergy of churches in a particular geographical area form a presbytery. Presbyteries in a region comprise a synod. All the synods of a wide area form the General Assembly. This is a "presbyterian" form of polity (church government) because presbyteries are the governing units that exercise direct authority over churches.

Presbyterian polity is grounded in principles that emphasize the unity of the church; its government by "presbyters," traditionally called ruling and teaching elders; and the commitment to governing bodies made up of presbyters meeting together in graduated units to the General Assembly level. Presbyters who govern are to seek the will of Christ and to decide by vote, after discussion, and through majority rule. The decisions of lower governing bodies can be reviewed by higher bodies. Presbyters are ordained only through a governing body and exercise shared power in governing the church through governing bodies. The church's Constitution is administered through the governing bodies, which maintain a mutuality of relationships among the various church structures. Presbyterians believe this governing system is established in accord with Scripture and exists to further good order in the church while seeking to be open to God's ongoing work in the church and in human history.

87. What is ordination?

Ordination is an action of the whole church in which a person is set apart to carry out certain ministries. Presbyterians recognize ordination for ministers of the Word and Sacrament and for elders and deacons. Ordination does not make an indelible "character change" in a person, giving a person any "special qualities." Instead, it is a recognition of the gifts of the Spirit bestowed on persons, and the call of God through the church for them to orient themselves to specific ministries of leadership in various settings.

Presbyterians have emphasized the need for preparation for ordination. Those ordained as ministers of the Word have been required to have theological education. They are required to have a relationship with the appropriate presbytery committee and to follow the specific directives established for them. Ordination in the Presbyterian tradition is always related to a prior "call" for service in the church. So ordination is to a specific call, recognized by the church as a valid ministry. Those ordained submit themselves to the church's confessional standards and to its discipline, promising to carry out their ministries in obedience to the church.

Those ordained to the offices of elders and deacons also generally receive some preparatory training to become acquainted with the specific duties and functions of these offices. They are ordained on the basis of the "call" of the congregation to these specific ministries, usually for a set period of time. They function in roles of governance and service, also submitting themselves to the church's confessional standards and its forms of church discipline.

Ordination is a ceremony held in the context of a worship service, usually featuring the apostolic practice of the "laying on of hands" (Acts 6:6; 8:18) to set apart the ordinand for ministry. The service of ordination is carried out on behalf of the whole church for specific ministerial functions. The service should also be a reminder or mirror for the whole assembled congregation that God gives spiritual gifts to all believers in Jesus Christ (1 Cor. 12) and the responsibility for each church member to exercise these gifts and to use them for "the common good" (1 Cor. 12:7). Those who are ordained have special, visible responsibilities in the church. They carry these out through offices in the church, prompting all church members to reflect on their own gifts and the ministries to which they are called.

88. What are elders and what do they do?

Traditionally the term "elder" in Presbyterian churches refers either to a "teaching elder"—the minister of Word and Sacrament—or to a "ruling elder," who is a layperson ordained to this office in a local congregation.

"Elder" is a term stretching back to Old Testament times, when the people of Israel were governed by elders (Ex. 3:16; 1 Sam. 8:4). In the New Testament, persons with special gifts shared in governing and ministries in local churches (Acts 15:4; Titus 1:5). The word "elder" is an English translation of the Greek term *presbyteros,* as found in the New Testament. So a "presbyterian" church is a church governed by elders.

Ruling elders are elected by the congregation and have responsibilities for leadership, government, and discipline in local churches and in other governing bodies, such as presbyteries, synods, and the General Assembly, to which they are elected as commissioners. In these bodies, ruling elders participate and vote in parity with teaching elders. Collectively, the body of ruling elders who exercise oversight over local congregations is called the session.

The duties of the elders are to strengthen and nurture Christian faith in congregations and to exercise spiritual oversight over the life and work of the church. Particularly they work with the pastor for the ordering of public worship and for equipping the congregation for ministries to the world. Special circumstances may lead to elders' being able to perform ministerial functions as authorized by a presbytery.

Ruling elders have exemplary duties and responsibilities by virtue of their ordination and role in the life of the church. They are to lead the congregation in enacting the law of love as they support the mission and ministry of the church through its worship, education, and service.

Further specific duties of the session are enumerated in different Presbyterian denominations. The pastor of a church serves as the moderator of the session. Many Presbyterian churches also have deacons (ordained) and trustees (nonordained) to carry out their distinctive functions. In some churches, elders also assume the duties of deacons and/or trustees.

89. What are deacons and what do they do?

Deacons are a New Testament office in the church and are charged with ministries of care, witness, and service. In the early church, deacons took on functions of this nature (Acts 6:1–6; 1 Tim. 3:8–13; 5:9–10; Rom. 12:8; 16:1–2). Concerns for the poor and those who suffer are primary. Deacons are ordained by the church to carry out these ministries and to lead the church institutionally in its mission and ministries in these areas. Presbyterians have seen deacons as a permanent office in the church to be present in all local congregations. In some churches today, though, elders on the session also function as deacons.

The ministry of service (Gr. *diakonia,* from which the term "deacon" is derived) is a ministry given to all Christians. But within the church, the institutional expression of service in Jesus Christ is entrusted to those who are called to this special ministry. The work of deacons does not replace the individual service to others that is part of all Christian discipleship. Typically, duties of deacons include ministering to those in need, visiting the sick, and concern for all in distress. The range of action for deacons should be both within the local congregation and beyond the community of faith to the culture in which the church is set. An extension of these concerns, consistent with the biblical office and Presbyterian tradition, is for deacons to lead the congregation in concerns for justice and peace as well as in individual acts of charity. The ordination of deacons is a particular reminder to all church members of their callings to service and to the responsibility to extend care to those in need.

In the past, some Presbyterian churches have limited the role of ruling elder to males. In most Presbyterian churches in the United States this practice has now changed. But the office of deacon has been a ministry women have fulfilled, recalling the mention of Phoebe in the church at Cenchreae (Rom. 16:1).

Other Christian churches have often regarded the office of deacon as an appropriate sacramental office, giving deacons responsibilities for preaching and administration in the Lord's Supper. While on occasion deacons in some Presbyterian churches may serve the Lord's Supper in the absence of elders, the office has been focused on meeting human needs and bringing the consciousness of such needs to the view of the congregation.

90. What is a presbytery and what does it do?

The presbytery is a governing body in a Presbyterian denomination that is comprised of all churches and ministers of Word and

Sacrament in a certain area. Presbyteries hold meetings in which churches are represented by ruling elders and ministers of the Word. A parity between the number of elders and ministers is usually sought. Elders and ministers are equal in their status to participate and vote in presbyteries.

Presbyteries are a core unit of the Presbyterian church government system. They are the governing bodies that deal with the immediate concerns of local congregations and are the bodies to which ministers of Word and Sacrament belong, instead of to local churches.

Presbyteries carry out many duties and responsibilities, through committees. They focus on leading churches in mission and ministries, coordinating church efforts, providing resources for local churches, giving pastoral care to churches and members of presbyteries, overseeing churches without pastors, ordaining ministers of Word and Sacrament, and carrying out church discipline as needed, among other functions. The presbytery has oversight of the records of local congregations. It continues to relate to higher governing bodies and to elect commissioners to serve in these bodies. It validates the ministries of its minister members, receives and dismisses those who enter and leave pastoral positions, and deals also with issues of church property, which in Presbyterian polity is owned not by a local church but by the presbytery.

Presbyteries vary widely in terms of their frequency of meeting. The ongoing work of presbyteries is usually carried on by staff personnel, who work with the presbytery committees. A moderator of the presbytery is elected annually to preside over presbytery meetings, and a stated clerk serves to keep necessary records, carry out correspondence, and interpret the church's Constitution.

Presbyteries may present "overtures" or "memorials" (in some Presbyterian bodies) to the General Assembly that suggest changes to the church's Constitution or practices. If approved by the Assembly, these items in some cases must be voted on by the presbyteries before changes take effect. Presbyteries, as other governing bodies, reflect the principle of representative government that is a feature of Presbyterian polity.

91. What is a General Assembly and what does it do?

The General Assembly is the highest governing body in Presbyterian churches. It represents the unity of the church through the other governing bodies: synods, presbyteries, and sessions of local congregations.

Presbyterian denominations use different formulas to allocate the number of delegates or commissioners to General Assembly. Usually there is an equal number of elders and ministers from each presbytery. The Assembly typically meets once per year, or once every two years.

The General Assembly speaks to the whole denomination. Among the main responsibilities and powers of General Assemblies are usually: to establish priorities and directions for the churches' ministries in Christ; to provide program functions for carrying out the church's mission; to establish and administer the church's ministries on a national and international scale; and to provide further services for the whole denomination. Many other duties and responsibilities as well are part of the work of General Assemblies.

Since the General Assembly is the highest governing body, it has an authoritative voice in many matters. Judicial cases involving matters of church discipline can move through the judicial system to the General Assembly level. Major changes in a Presbyterian denomination—such as a change in the church's confessional standards—may be approved by a General Assembly, sent to presbyteries for vote, and then voted on at the next General Assembly. Presbyteries may send overtures or memorials to a General Assembly, with suggested changes to be considered.

The work of a General Assembly throughout a year is usually carried out by denominational staff as well as by those in leadership in synods and presbyteries. The Assembly is the means by which the denomination corresponds with other churches. The Stated Clerk of the General Assembly has responsibilities for interpreting the church's Constitution and may speak on behalf of the church during the course of a year. The Assembly is presided over by a Moderator, elected by the Assembly, to serve as a spokesperson for the church during the period until a new Moderator is elected at the next General Assembly.

92. What is church discipline and why is it important?

Church discipline is a part of the church's life to enhance the honor of God among church members. The Presbyterian and Reformed tradition has always seen church discipline as important. The Scots Confession (1560) listed it along with the preaching of the Word of God and the right administration of the sacraments as one of the three crucial elements that define a church.

Church discipline seeks to honor God by making clear what church membership means. Discipline attempts to correct and restrain wrongdoing by those in the church, to remove causes of discord and division in the church, and to restore wrongdoers to repentance and restoration while offering nourishment to them. These are theological motives, and church discipline is understood to emerge from the nature of God and the gospel of Jesus Christ. Church discipline is to serve positive purposes, even when difficult decisions or actions are carried out. Discipline should seek to build up the body of Christ (1 Cor. 10:23; 1 Thess. 5:11) and be exercised for purposes of redemption rather than punishment. Discipline should be enacted out of a concern for mercy rather than wrath. When the church needs to exercise discipline, it does so to strengthen the whole church and its unity. When difficulties arise, the church uses its established system of discipline to enact a suitable resolution.

Church discipline in the Presbyterian tradition features a judicial process that proceeds according to the Constitution of the specific Presbyterian denomination. The procedures are ecclesiastical, rather than civil. They are spelled out as exactly as possible to ensure justice, protection, and equity in dealing with issues that affect the purity of the church. A judicial process may be initiated for irregularities and delinquencies of governing bodies as well as for the prevention and correction of offenses committed by church members or officers. The four governing bodies (session, presbytery, synod, and General Assembly) are the places where the process is carried out and where appeals to decisions may be entered.

A basic principle of Presbyterian polity is that "truth is in order to goodness"* This means faith and practice must be related. So at times, the church must exercise its disciplinary oversight. When it does, however, the nature of the discipline should reflect the nature of the gospel. The goal must always be that believers "may be blameless on the day of our Lord Jesus Christ" (1 Cor. 1:8; Phil. 1:10).

---

*The Constitution of the Presbyterian Church (U.S.A.), Part II, Book of Order (Louisville, Ky.: Office of the General Assembly, 2002), G-1.0304.

For Further Reading

Angell, James W. *How to Spell Presbyterian*. Newly rev. ed. Louisville, Ky.: Geneva Press, 2002.

The Constitution of the Presbyterian Church (U.S.A.), Part I, *Book of Confessions*. Louisville, Ky.: Office of the General Assembly, 2002.

Calvin, John. *Institutes of the Christian Religion*. Ed. John T. McNeill. Trans. Ford Lewis Battles. Library of Christian Classics. 2 vols. Philadelphia: Westminster Press, 1960.

Gerstner, John H. *Theology for Everyman*. Chicago: Moody Press, 1965.

Guthrie, Shirley C. *Always Being Reformed: Faith for a Fragmented World*. Louisville, Ky.: Westminster John Knox Press, 1996.

————. *Christian Doctrine*. Rev. ed. Louisville, Ky.: Westminster John Knox Press, 1994.

Johnson, Earl S., Jr. *Witness without Parallel: Eight Biblical Texts That Make Us Presbyterian*. Louisville, Ky.: Geneva Press, 2003.

Leitch, Addison H. *A Layman's Guide to Presbyterian Beliefs*. Grand Rapids: Zondervan Publishing House, 1967.

Leith, John H. *Introduction to the Reformed Tradition: A Way of Being the Christian Community*. Atlanta: John Knox Press, 1980.

Lingle, Walter L., and John W. Kuykendall. *Presbyterians: Their History and Beliefs*. 4th rev. ed. Atlanta: John Knox Press, 1978.

McKim, Donald K. *Introducing the Reformed Faith: Biblical Revelation, Christian Tradition, Contemporary Significance*. Louisville, Ky.: Westminster John Knox Press, 2001.

————. *Presbyterian Beliefs: A Brief Introduction*. Louisville, Ky.: Geneva Press, 2003.

————, ed. *Calvin's* Institutes: *Abridged Edition*. Louisville, Ky.: Westminster John Knox Press, 2001.

————, ed. *The Westminster Handbook to Reformed Theology*. Louisville, Ky.: Westminster John Knox Press, 2001.

Plunkett, Stephen W. *This We Believe: Eight Truths Presbyterians Affirm*. Louisville, Ky.: Geneva Press, 2002.

Rogers, Jack. *Presbyterian Creeds: A Guide to the Book of Confessions*. Louisville, Ky.: Westminster Press, 1991.

————. *Reading the Bible and the Confessions: The Presbyterian Way.* Louisville, Ky.: Geneva Press, 1999.

Rohls, Jan. *Reformed Confessions: Theology from Zurich to Barmen.* Trans. John Hoffmeyer. Columbia Series in Reformed Theology. Louisville, Ky.: Westminster John Knox Press, 1998.

Weeks, Louis B. *The Presbyterian Source: Bible Words That Shape a Faith.* Louisville, Ky.: Westminster/John Knox Press, 1990.

————. *To Be a Presbyterian.* Atlanta: John Knox Press, 1983.